JEN BEE

Card Crafting

Card Crafting

Over 45 Ideas for Making Greeting Cards & Stationery

Gillian Souter

 Sterling Publishing Co., Inc.   New York

❖ Acknowledgments ❖

My thanks to those friends who, for inspiration, volunteered cards they had long treasured. I am indebted to Kathy Mossop for all the advice and support she gave, and to Liz Gill and Carol Knox for their constructive suggestions. Special thanks to Barry Eggleton, who provided the line-drawings and to John who provided the sustenance!

Library of Congress Cataloging-in-Publication Data Available

Graphic Design: Barry Eggleton
Pattern Drawings: Gillian Souter
Photography: Robert Fretwell

10 9 8 7 6 5 4 3 2 1

First published in the United States in 1992
by Sterling Publishing Company, Inc.
387 Park Avenue South, New York, N.Y. 10016
Originally published in Australia in 1991
by Off the Shelf Publishing
32 Thomas Street, Lewisham NSW 2049
Text and designs ⓒ 1991 by Gillian Souter
Distributed in Canada by Sterling Publishing
c/o Canadian Manda Group, P.O. Box 920, Station U
Toronto, Ontario, Canada M8Z 5P9
Distributed in Great Britain and Europe by Cassell PLC
Villiers House, 41/47 Strand, London WC2N 5JE, England
Printed in Hong Kong

Sterling ISBN 0-8069-8682-4

❖ ❖ ❖ **Contents** ❖ ❖ ❖

Projects for special occasions
page viii

Introduction   page 1

1 Materials & Equipment   page 3
❖ Paper and card ❖ Cutting equipment ❖ Other equipment ❖

2 Basic Techniques   page 7
❖ Handling paper ❖ Transferring patterns ❖ Ruling lines ❖ Cutting and scoring ❖
❖ Basic shapes ❖ Mounting finished work ❖ Multiple copies of cards ❖

3 Tags & Envelopes   page 15

4 Papermaking   page 19
❖ Equipment ❖ Materials ❖ Making the paper ❖
❖ Adding color and objects ❖ Varying shape and texture ❖

5 Lettering   page 27
❖ Materials ❖ Forming letters ❖ Spacing ❖ The message ❖
❖ Double thanks ❖ True-love knot ❖

6 Cut-outs   page 35
❖ Window box ❖ Stained glass ❖ Natural perspective ❖
❖ Cut-and-twist figures ❖ Advent card ❖

7 Paper Appliqué   page 47
❖ Traditional approaches ❖ Raised découpage ❖ Wildflower collages ❖
❖ Déchirage squares ❖ Laminated shapes ❖ Tissue lambs ❖

8 Weaving page 55
❖ Satin checkerboard ❖ Pierced heart ❖
❖ Ribbon weave ❖ Christmas tree ❖

9 Paper Sculpture page 63
❖ Sculpted flowers ❖ Starburst ❖ Pop-up swan ❖
❖ Clear impressions ❖ Embossed letters ❖

10 Painting page 71
❖ Paste painting ❖ Spattering ❖ Salt and silk ❖
❖ Marbling ❖

11 Printing page 79
❖ Leaf prints ❖ Eraser prints ❖ Ball mum lino-cut ❖
❖ Zodiac stencil ❖ Spring blossom stencil ❖

12 Needlecraft page 91
❖ Materials ❖ Geometric curves ❖ Satin tulips ❖
❖ Bargello heart ❖ Cross-stitch butterfly ❖

13 Photo Images page 99
❖ Framed photos ❖ Tinted pictures ❖ Photograms ❖

14 Quilling page 107
❖ Materials ❖ Chickens ❖ Snowflake ❖
❖ Quilled hearts ❖ Sailing boat ❖ Basic quilling shapes ❖

15 Cards & Kids page 115
❖ Materials ❖ Adapting a card craft ❖ Potato prints ❖
❖ Marble trails ❖ Drop-dyes ❖ Crayon-rubbings ❖

Metric Equivalents

INCHES TO MILLIMETRES AND CENTIMETRES

MM—millimetres   *CM—centimetres*

Inches	MM	CM	Inches	CM	Inches	CM
1/8	3	0.3	9	22.9	30	76.2
1/4	6	0.6	10	25.4	31	78.7
3/8	10	1.0	11	27.9	32	81.3
1/2	13	1.3	12	30.5	33	83.8
5/8	16	1.6	13	33.0	34	86.4
3/4	19	1.9	14	35.6	35	88.9
7/8	22	2.2	15	38.1	36	91.4
1	25	2.5	16	40.6	37	94.0
1 1/4	32	3.2	17	43.2	38	96.5
1 1/2	38	3.8	18	45.7	39	99.1
1 3/4	44	4.4	19	48.3	40	101.6
2	51	5.1	20	50.8	41	104.1
2 1/2	64	6.4	21	53.3	42	106.7
2	76	7.6	22	55.9	43	109.2
3 1/2	89	8.9	23	58.4	44	111.8
4	102	10.2	24	61.0	45	114.3
4 1/2	114	11.4	25	63.5	46	116.8
5	127	12.7	26	66.0	47	119.4
6	152	15.2	27	68.6	48	121.9
7	178	17.8	28	71.1	49	124.5
8	203	20.3	29	73.7	50	127.0

Projects for special occasions ❖ ❖

Most of the projects in this book can be adapted for any festivity or occasion, perhaps by simply changing the colors or the motif. Some cards, however, are particularly well-suited to events we traditionally celebrate. The number after the project is the chapter in which you will find it.

Anniversary	Cut-and-twist numbers 6
Baby's arrival	Tissue lambs 7; Satin tulips 12; Framed photo 13; Quilled chicks 14
Birthday	Cut-and-twist numbers 6; Zodiac stencil 11
Bon voyage	Sailing boat 14
Christmas	Stained glass 6; Advent card 6; Wildflower collage 7; Woven tree 8; Starburst 9; Snowflake 14; Potato prints 15
Easter	Stained glass 6; Tissue lambs 7; Quilled chicks 14
Father's day	Déchirage squares 7; Graphed threads 12; Sailing boat 14
Get well	Window box 6
Marriage	Satin tulips 12; Bargello heart 12
Mother's day	Raised découpage 7; Sculpted flowers 9; Bargello heart 12; Quilled hearts 14
Season's greetings	Embossed letters 9
St Valentine's day	True-love knot 5; Raised découpage 7; Pierced heart 8; Bargello heart 12; Quilled hearts 14
Thank you	Double thanks 5

Introduction ❖ ❖ ❖ ❖ ❖ ❖ ❖ ❖ ❖ ❖ ❖ ❖ ❖

Card crafting is a pastime I've enjoyed now for many years. I took it up with a vengeance when I got fed up with the poor range of cards available commercially and vowed never to buy another greeting card, but to make them instead. These days the choice is much improved and I do occasionally break that promise, but there are still plenty of reasons to keep it.

The first is, quite simply, the cost. The high price of a good card is hardly an encouragement to stock up for those approaching birthdays. (It's odd that cards which display a degree of good taste are apparently so much more expensive to manufacture.) The home-made card can cost little more than your time.

Your time and thought makes each card far more valuable than any bought in a shop. Think how much you appreciate a personalized birthday card or a simple handmade card at Christmas. These things are a measure of much affection.

The last motive is a more selfish one. You can gain a lot of satisfaction from making anything, even as small a thing as a greeting card. Using your hands and imagination in something different from your normal occupation can be relaxing and, for those of us who are artistic to only a modest degree, highly rewarding.

This book will introduce you to a variety of crafts through small-scale and manageable projects. You will undoubtedly want to explore some of these methods further and, if you do, you will have the pleasure of discovering countless new designs and new applications.

1 Materials & Equipment ❖❖❖❖❖❖

Personally, I find art supplies and stationery irresistible and am always looking for some excuse to indulge in such items. This book offers you that excuse: the different techniques use various bits and pieces. On the other hand, most of the materials and equipment are inexpensive and many can be found in the home.

Each project includes a list of the items required, so check this before you begin. This chapter lists the basic things you will need and most of these are shown in the picture opposite.

Paper and card

Paper and card are really one and the same; card simply refers to thicker or sturdier paper. A thick or heavy paper or a card stock will make a good greeting card, but if you have lightweight paper that you like, glue two pieces together to form a stronger material. If you use different colors, this can add to your design. Alternatively, you can use a French fold (see Chapter 2) to make a stronger card structure.

An array of papers

Thickness is only one of the ways papers can differ. Though most paper is made of wood pulp, some contains cotton for added strength while others may contain strands of silk or pieces of leaf matter to add interest. Paper can have a gloss or matt finish, it can be plain or decorated, and can have a coarse or smooth texture.

Paper is also available in sheets of different sizes. A good way of saving some time is to buy sheets of stiff writing paper which simply need to be folded to give a card format. However, the more interesting types of paper are generally only available in larger sheets which will need to be cut. When choosing paper, consider what will be most efficient and economical.

Ideally, you will have an array of textures and colors at hand, so that your options aren't limited when you want to make a card. Some art supply shops and stationers stock books of art paper; these can be an economical way of buying good paper in a range of colors. No matter how you decorate your card, the paper is the most important part. It is worth spending money on paper and improvising on implements and other materials instead.

Cutting equipment

As so much of card crafting is in the cutting, you will need a good sharp knife. Craft knives with retractable and replaceable blades are ideal. Commercial artists use scalpels with very fine blades which are difficult to change. Whichever you choose, replace the blade regularly so that cuts are sharply made. If you can't retract the blade on your knife, keep it safely stuck in a cork or eraser.

Another essential item is a good cutting surface. Thick cardboard can be used but it will have a short life span. Masonite lasts longer but tends to blunt the knife. The best surface is a self-healing cutting mat, available from art supply shops. These often have a grid printed on them which can help when measuring up cards.

Cut straight lines against a metal ruler rather than one made of wood or plastic, as a sharp knife can easily slice into these. You will also need a set square to rule right-angles.

Some projects require scissors; keep one pair for paper and another for fabric, as cutting paper blunts the blades. A pair of small manicure scissors is also useful for fine work.

Adhesives

Many of the cards featured in this book were made using double-sided adhesive tape which is easier to handle than glue. Once used, however, it is difficult to move items so position them with care. Removable one-sided tape is very useful for holding paper and stencils in place while positioning them.

Standard white glue gives a very strong bond but may wrinkle thin papers. I prefer craft glue, a variant which is not as strong but dries faster.

Using a spray adhesive (without chlorofluorocarbons) is an efficient way of gluing large items together. Use only in a well-ventilated room and, to prevent making a mess, place the item to be glued in a cardboard box and spray into the box. If the nozzle becomes clogged, tip the can upside down and spray briefly.

Other equipment

You will need a pencil for drawing guide lines and transferring designs. Leads vary from H (hard) to B (soft); choose one between HB and 2B. A drafting or lay-out pencil, which is rectangular in cross-section, is useful for practising lettering. Felt-tipped pens of different thickness are useful for writing your message and for some decoration. Gold and silver marker pens are especially useful for writing on dark card.

Paints come in a bewildering variety. For nearly all the projects in this book, a water-based paint is recommended. (The exception is marbling which requires cheap oil paints.) Acrylic paint comes in tubes or tubs and is easy to use. When dry, it is waterproof so you must wash brushes in water immediately after use. Watercolors are available in tubes or hard cakes and give a translucent and subtle effect. Gouache, which is used by commercial artists, is an opaque water-based paint which is thin and creamy and very good for painting fine detail. Powder and poster paints are more economical and suitable for bright designs.

It is handy to have a variety of brushes, from fine watercolor brushes to heavy household ones. A toothbrush is suitable for some projects. An eraser is essential. Keep it clean by rubbing it on clean scrap paper when necessary. Spare erasers can be used as printing blocks (see Chapter 11). You will need some paper for transferring patterns. A strong translucent paper can be bought from art supply shops but household greaseproof is cheaper. Other useful items are toothpicks, skewers, a roller or brayer (shown in the top right of the photograph), two boards for pressing cards and paper, a holepunch, and the lid of an ice-cream tub for rolling paint.

Satin ribbons can make a card special, while curling ribbon adds a festive touch. Be on the look-out for interesting bits of lace, buttons, glitter and so on. Natural objects, such as flowers, seeds, and leaves can add a rustic charm to your cards.

2 Basic Techniques ❖ ❖ ❖ ❖ ❖ ❖ ❖ ❖ ❖ ❖

A major part of card crafting is learning how to manipulate paper effectively. This includes mastering the basic techniques of measuring and cutting: a badly cut card spoils any decoration. Some of the projects in this book require you to cut the card structure first and then decorate it; others suggest you make the design and then cut a suitable card around it. When attempting a new method, think carefully about the most suitable sequence.

Handling paper

Store paper flat if at all possible; if you don't have room to do this, roll it very loosely. Try to keep it in a dry place where the temperature is moderate. Always handle paper with clean, dry hands and lift large sheets carefully so they do not buckle.

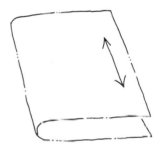

Most paper has a grain: all fibres lie in one direction. It is useful to identify the grain direction as a card will fold flatter if cut **with** the grain rather than **against** it. (Note that if you are making a pop-up card you may want your card to stay open, so you would fold it against the grain.) To determine the grain direction, place the sheet on a flat surface and roll one side to meet the other, release it, then roll the bottom to meet the top. Whichever roll gives the least resistance is the direction of the grain. The arrows in the diagram indicate this clearly.

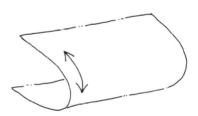

There is no correct side to paper, though one side has sometimes received more sizing or coating than the other. Work on whichever one you think is more attractive.

The arrows indicate the direction of the grain

Transferring patterns

Transferring a motif is a three-stage process using tracing or greaseproof paper, a pencil and some removable tape.

❖ Place the paper over the pattern and tape it in place.
❖ Draw over the lines of the pattern.
❖ Remove the tracing and scribble over the back of it with pencil.
❖ Position the tracing on your card, scribbled-side down, and draw over the lines of the pattern once again. The pattern should now appear on the card underneath.

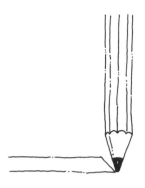

Ruling a line

Ruling lines

Before cutting a card, it may help to rule faint guide lines in pencil. To do so, place the ruler as close as possible to the points being joined and hold the pencil at a right angle to the paper.

After you have ruled many such lines, pencil lead can build up on your ruler. Wipe the edge occasionally so that it doesn't mark your work.

Cutting and scoring

The cleanest cuts are made with a firm hand, but don't apply too much pressure to the knife or it will drag the fibres of the paper and leave a wrinkled edge. You may need to run the knife a second time, especially if cutting a double thickness of card.

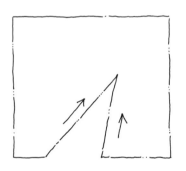

Cutting a sharp angle

Where possible, align paper so that if you slip you will cut into the waste material, rather than the piece you wish to use. When cutting a sharp angle, cut on each side towards the point as shown in the diagram. You will find it easier to cut curved lines if you hold the knife as a pen, taking great care as your fingers are less protected.

Consider tearing paper instead of cutting; the ragged edge created can provide an interesting texture. Tearing across the grain will provide an even more ragged edge.

A score is a half-cut, that is, one which only breaks the top fibres of the card, allowing it to fold more crisply. How heavily you need to press depends on the thickness of the paper and on the sharpness of the blade; it may be worthwhile practicing on scrap first. Score on the outside of your planned card, so that the paper bends away from the line to form two panels.

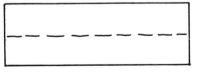

Lines of dashes indicate score lines

NOTE: Throughout the patterns in this book, I have used a line of dashes to indicate a score mark, while a heavy line shows you where to make a cut.

Basic shapes

When choosing a shape for your card, keep in mind:
* ❖ the size of your envelope
* ❖ postage restrictions
* ❖ whether you want the card to stand up
* ❖ the age of the person who will receive it
* ❖ the length of your message

Greeting cards are generally folded so that they can stand. The most common format is a "portrait" shape with a single fold along the long edge and opening on the right, though this shape may be turned so that the fold is at the top. A "landscape" format is one folded along the short edge, so it tends to be a less stable structure. One fold will normally make cardboard or thick paper rigid enough to stand, but if you use thin paper you might fold it twice in a French fold.

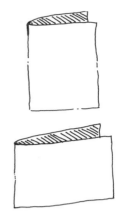

Portrait and landscape cards

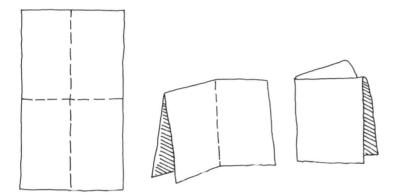

A French fold

Folds can be used to add interest as well as strength to a card. A concertina card is one folded first one way and then another. Greeting cards can also be cut in interesting shapes - perhaps a house for a new home or a ring for an engagement - but remember to leave a folded edge to hinge the front and back of the card together.

Some unusual shapes for cards

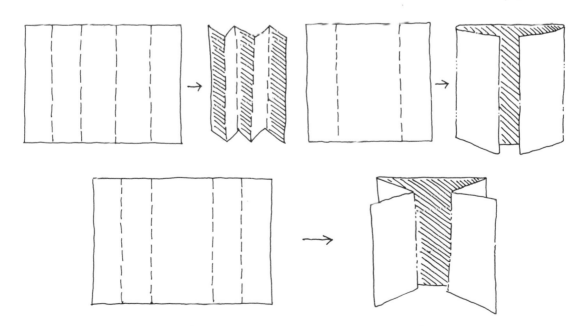

To make a blank two-panel card, measure and cut a rectangular piece of card twice the size of your planned front panel. Make a pencil mark halfway along the two long edges and score between these two points. Fold along the scored line and gently press the card flat. You may find that the angles are crooked. If so, close the card and trim through both panels along the top and bottom edges so that they are at right angles to the scored edge, then trim the opening edge.

Making a two-panel card

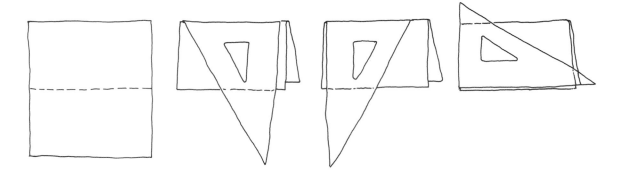

Windows in three-panel mounts

If you wish to frame pictures or embroidery neatly, use a three-panel mount. Blank cards like these are available from most craft shops, but they are easy to make. Choose a size for the front panel and multiply the width by three. Mark the cutting and scoring lines on a piece of card in pencil. On the middle panel, mark and cut a window to fit your piece of work. You may need to trim the edge of one panel so that the card folds flat.

Don't restrict yourself to rectangular windows: use a template (or draw freehand) different shapes such as ovals, circles, hearts and so on. On the next page, you will find the template for a mount shown in Chapter 10; use it to mount attractive wrapping paper or paper you have decorated yourself.

If your sheet of card is not large enough to make a three-panel card, cut a two-panel one along with a single panel in another color, which can then be glued or taped in place. This is sometimes necessary if you wish to mount thin paper or fabric in a dark card; a white backing panel will prevent the dark card showing through and spoiling your work.

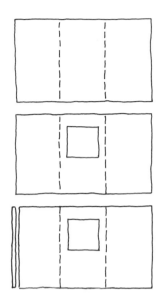

A three-panel mount from inside

Photocopied cards

Pattern for an unusual three-panel window

Mounting finished work

To mount something directly on the front of a two-panel card, dot glue on the corners of the item or run double-sided tape along each edge, then position it on the front panel and press down. Don't spread glue all over; it might warp the paper or card and leave wrinkles.

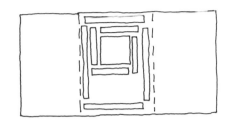

To mount your work in a three-panel card, first trim it so it is ½ or 1 in larger each way than the window. On the inside of the middle panel, dot some glue or stick strips of double-sided tape around the window and along the edges of the panel. Place your work carefully so that it is centered in the window and then fold over the narrow panel and press.

A good way of preventing a large piece of embroidery or decorated paper from rippling when mounted is to spray adhesive onto the back of it, before pressing down the backing panel.

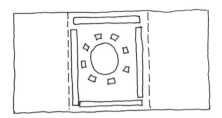

Positioning tape on the middle panel for mounting work

Multiple copies of cards

Everyone who has had to rush out and buy a last minute card would appreciate that it is good to have a stock of them ready-made. When you try the different methods in this book, I suggest you make more than one card, as much of the time is spent setting up and then clearing away. Some of the techniques, such as printing, marbling and making photograms, are ideal for making multiple copies.

To save time, consider photocopying a monotone design onto colored paper. If you draw the outline of a motif or letters in black pen, you can hand-color photocopies so they still appear personalized. Alternatively, color photocopying is becoming less and less expensive.

Those with access to and ability with a computer might consider using a drawing program to design a simple motif and set a perfect message. Keep in mind, though, that a computer can't do your designing for you and that cards produced on them might look a little impersonal.

If you want a very large number of cards, contact an instant printer and enquire about methods to suit your particular requirements.

3 Tags & Envelopes ❖ ❖ ❖ ❖ ❖ ❖ ❖ ❖ ❖ ❖

Gift tags are the simplest form of card - a flat surface decorated on one or both sides, with a thread or ribbon attached. As they don't need to stand upright, they can be cut in any shape to reflect the occasion or the person for whom the gift is intended.

Some of the decorative techniques described in this book, such as marbling, spattering, paste painting or printing, are also well suited to making wrapping paper. If you have made or bought a particularly attractive wrapping paper, consider making a matching card or gift tag from an offcut.

To attach a tag ribbon:
❖ Punch or cut a hole in a corner of the tag.
❖ Cut a suitable length of ribbon and fold it in half.
❖ Pull the ribbon part of the way through the hole to form a loop.
❖ Thread the two ends through the loop and pull tight.
❖ Tie the ends to the wrapped gift so that the tag hangs loosely.

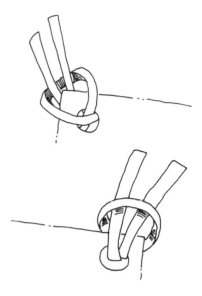

A tag ribbon seen from both sides

Homemade envelopes

Always plan your card with your envelope in mind. However, if a suitable sized envelope is not commercially available, you can tailor-make your own. Patterns are given for two types; your choice could be dictated by the size of your sheet of card. All the flaps can be sealed with glue, but you might seal the last flap with an attractive sticker or cut slits so that it self-seals.

Three-dimensional cards, such as quilled and sculpted ones, are safer sent in a shallow but strong box. The acetate boxes which hold handkerchiefs or stationery are ideal. Remember to check postal restrictions on size and shape of envelopes.

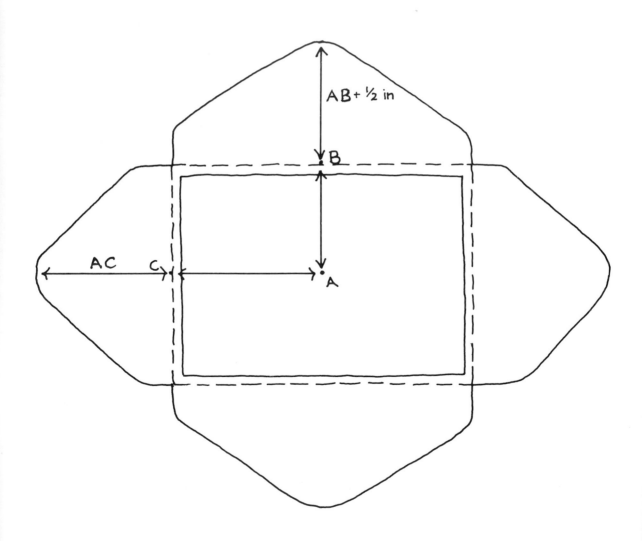

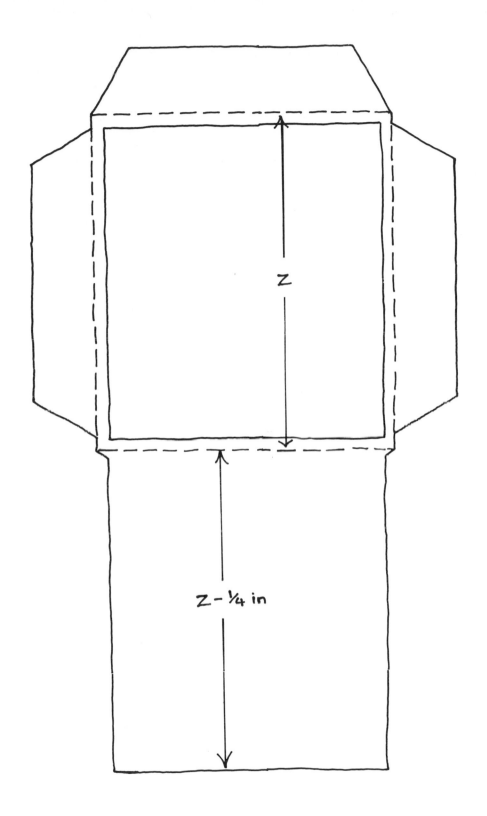

Greeting cards made from recycled paper

4 Papermaking ❖ ❖ ❖ ❖ ❖ ❖ ❖ ❖ ❖ ❖ ❖ ❖

None of the projects in this book would be possible if we did not have paper. Indeed, the whole notion of a cheap and portable written message was not really possible until paper had been invented. This happened relatively late in our history. The people of ancient Egypt wove papyrus reeds together and beat them into a flat hard sheet; Pacific islanders beat bark into thin sheets; but it was not until AD 105 that a Chinese court eunuch named Ts'ai Lun registered the basic method that we know today.

Paper is simply a layer of intertwined fibres. These fibres can come from various natural sources which are soaked and beaten to produce a pulp of loose fibres. A screen (the mold and deckle) is dipped into a mixture of pulp and water and then drained. The resulting sheet of fibres is transferred from the mold onto a couch of cloth to drain, then pressed between boards and, finally, hung to dry.

The increased demand for paper eventually led to the establishment of paper-mills and most of the paper we see today has the sharp edges and smooth finish of the manufactured product. Though this is obviously more suitable for business purposes, it doesn't have the character and fine qualities of a good handmade paper, which contains no bleaches and has no directional grain. Handmade paper generally preserves better too; cards that you make on handmade paper and store carefully would probably outlast the pages of this book.

The most common source of fibre for commercial paper production is wood, and the quantity now required for everyday use is creating environmental and economic problems. Whether or not you make your own paper will hardly affect the rate of forest depletion in the world, but it will allow you and your friends to glimpse the possibilities of recycling.

The simplest but strongest reason for making your own paper is the pure enjoyment of it. Once you have bought or made the few pieces of equipment, there is very little extra expense. When you have learnt the basic procedures, there is a great deal of room for experimentation and individuality. And there are few things more satisfying than removing the boards of your press to find that your efforts have been rewarded.

Greeting cards can be made by merely folding a piece of handmade paper and letting it speak for itself. Try making a collage of different colored papers or select a piece which has been embossed or flower-studded. If papermaking becomes a regular pastime, you can use your own product as the basis for other card crafts. Any way you use it, it will be valued immensely.

Equipment

The most important piece of equipment is the flat sieve, which comes in two parts: the mold and the deckle. The mold is a rectangular wooden frame which has wire or nylon mesh stretched tight across it. The deckle is a frame of the same size but with no mesh; it traps the pulp on the mold and gives handmade paper its distinctive edges.

A mold and deckle

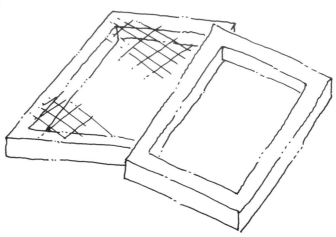

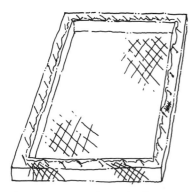

Assemble the frame

You can buy an inexpensive mold and deckle from selected craft shops; if you have trouble finding a supplier, a conservation organization may be able to direct you. Alternatively, you can make your own. The following measurements will produce 8½ x 11 in paper.

- ❖ Saw a length of ¾ in square wood into 8 pieces: 4 of them measuring 9¼ in and the other 4 measuring 11¾ in.
- ❖ Arrange them as in the diagram and secure them with screws, nails, or more permanently with brass corner braces.
- ❖ Cut a 14½ x 16½ in piece of nylon mesh which has between 30 and 50 holes per in.
- ❖ Dampen the mesh and then staple or tack it taut along one edge of a frame before stretching it tightly across and securing it at the other edge. Still pulling it taut, secure it along the other edges.
- ❖ Trim the excess mesh away.

You will also need two boards for pressing layers of pulp. Laminated boards are ideal because they will not warp when wet. These can either be weighted with bricks or clamped together with several C-clamps. If you do have clamps, this will allow you to prop the press at an angle for better drainage.

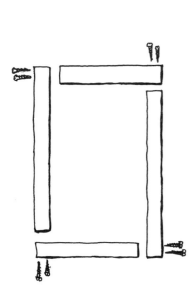

Secure the mesh on the frame

A blender offers a quick way of breaking up fibres into pulp. If you do not have one, you can pound soaked material into a pulp using a heavy piece of wood and a bucket.

The basin for holding the pulp and water mixture must be large enough to hold the mold lying flat, otherwise your paper will be uneven. A sink can be used, but be careful to strain the leftover mixture before removing the plug.

Materials

Paper can be made from any fibrous material: the more densely packed it is, the more effort will be required to break it down. Cotton rag, the main ingredient used in papermaking until demand overtook supply, makes a very strong paper but needs to be soaked for up to a month before it can be pulped. Herbaceous plants such as grass, ferns, celery and so on, have no woody tissue and can be boiled into a soggy pulp which will make coarsely textured paper.

The most straightforward source of fibre is waste paper - envelopes, computer paper, paper bags, wrapping paper - anything that is not too heavily inked or coated. Newspaper can be added as bulk but paper made from it lacks strength and will not last as long. The color of your pulp will be determined by the paper you use, but don't strive for pure white paper; the shades of brown or grey produced by recycling printed paper have a more natural appearance.

You can buy cotton linters made for the purpose of strengthening handmade paper but they are relatively expensive. You might add some to a pulp of paper, but it is not necessary. Similarly, some of the coarser fibres mentioned above can be mixed with pulp from waste paper. Try different combinations to create a strong, attractive and functional paper.

Handmade paper is quite absorbent, which makes it suitable for printing but gives a feathery effect when you write on it in ink. Starch or gelatine can be used to seal or size the paper either by adding them to the pulp mixture or by dipping the finished paper in a prepared solution. If you choose to add gelatine before molding the paper, lumps may form unless you cool the solution before adding it to the pulp.

You will need a supply of cloths for laying down or couching each sheet of paper. Reusable kitchen cloths are easiest to use but some brands leave quite a heavy impression on the paper. Felt gives a very smooth finish and linen and cotton create a lovely texture.

Making the paper

You will need:
    a mold and deckle
    two pressing boards
    a blender
    an oblong basin
    pieces of cloth
    a towel
    a wooden spoon
    a sponge
    household starch
    newspaper
    waste paper

Your first effort may not be perfect, but you will find that you quickly learn to judge the consistency of the pulp and couch it smoothly. To ensure the best results, read through all the instructions before starting so that you have an overview of the process. Note that individual stages don't take much time, but you will need to leave an overnight gap between some stages.

❖ Sort your waste paper into different colors and remove any staples, sticky tape or plastic windows which will spoil the texture of your paper.
❖ Tear the paper into 1 in squares. Half a pound of waste paper will make between 10 and 20 sheets.
❖ Pour hot water over the scraps, stir to separate them, then leave the mixture to soak overnight.
❖ Mix 1 tablespoon of starch in hot water and stir to dissolve.
❖ Place a handful of soaked paper scraps in the blender and fill it two-thirds full with cold water.
❖ Blend the mixture for 15 seconds. If you can see lumps, blend for a little longer, but avoid blending too long or your paper will lack strength.
❖ Half-fill your basin with water, then add six batches of liquidized pulp.
❖ Set up a "couching mound": fold the towel to the same size as the mold, lay it flat with no creases, and lay a piece of damp cloth over it.
❖ Stir the pulp mixture immediately before dipping the mold; if the fibres settle on the bottom, your sheet will be very thin.
❖ Place the deckle on top of the mold, which should be mesh side up, and hold them firmly together with both hands.
Dip the mold and deckle vertically into the far side of the basin, then in one movement, level them under the surface and lift them straight up out of the pulp.

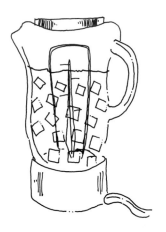

Liquidize the scraps in batches

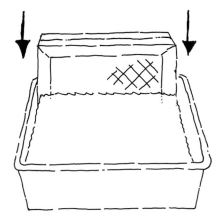

Dip the mold and deckle vertically

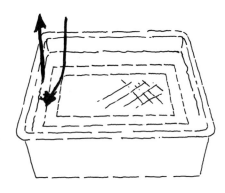

Immerse and level them, then lift

A range of papers made by adding plants and dye

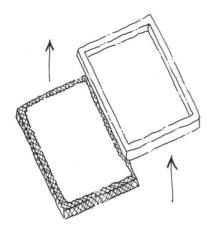

Lift the deckle from the mold

❖ While the water drains through the mesh, hold the mold and deckle horizontal and agitate them very gently from side to side and front to back. This evens out the pulp.
❖ Tilt the mold and deckle so any excess water runs off.
❖ Lay the mold on some newspaper and remove the deckle in one action so that no drips fall on the pulp and spoil it.
❖ The layer of pulp on the mold should be about $\frac{1}{16}$ in thick. If it looks too thin, add more pulp to the mixture and drain off some water. If it is too thick, add more water. Keep in mind that the mixture will become thinner as you form each sheet.
❖ Badly formed sheets can be returned to the mixture by re-dipping the mold.
❖ Invert the mold and hold it over your couching mound, then gently roll the pulp down onto the cloth.

Roll the mold onto the couching cloth

Press the layers between boards

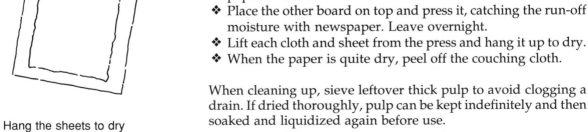

Hang the sheets to dry

❖ Leave the mold resting on the cloth and absorb excess moisture by pressing the back of the mesh with a sponge.
❖ Carefully roll the mold off, leaving the pulp on the cloth and watching that it does not stick at any point.
❖ Cover the pulp with another damp cloth, making sure there are no creases, and continue dipping and couching sheets.
❖ Cover the last sheet with a cloth and lift the layers of cloth and paper off the towel and onto one of the boards.
❖ Place the other board on top and press it, catching the run-off moisture with newspaper. Leave overnight.
❖ Lift each cloth and sheet from the press and hang it up to dry.
❖ When the paper is quite dry, peel off the couching cloth.

When cleaning up, sieve leftover thick pulp to avoid clogging a drain. If dried thoroughly, pulp can be kept indefinitely and then soaked and liquidized again before use.

Adding color and objects

The easiest way to color paper is to pulp scraps of one color, say, by using only envelopes with a blue lining. Alternatively, you can use food coloring, fabric dyes or water-based paints. Liquid dyes, such as food coloring, can simply be added to the pulp and water mixture in the basin. If you use powder paints or other heavily concentrated types of dye, add them when liquidizing the pulp so that they are evenly mixed.

The color of the pulp will darken when the paper dries: you can test it by taking a large pinch and drying it with a hairdryer. If you start with a white pulp and add dye progressively after forming each sheet, you will get more variety in one session.

You can also choose to keep the pulp a discreet white or brown and create interest by adding whole leaves, petals, seeds or other objects. Small items can be added to the pulp mixture and caught in the rising mold and deckle. Larger objects may need to be embedded: drain a sheet of pulp in the mold and deckle until it has stopped dripping, then gently press the object onto the sheet and dip into the pulp mixture again.

Embed objects by double-dipping

Fleshy plant matter, such as whole flower heads, should be pressed and dried first. Such objects will leave an impression in the whole stack of papers if separated only by thin couching cloths when pressed: use a towel or felt to avoid this.

To obtain a good impression of a veined leaf or feather, lay the object on a thick sheet of pulp which has been couched. Press as usual and then iron the paper and object between two cloths. Carefully remove the object once the paper is dry.

Impress paper while it is still damp

Varying shape and texture

An 8½ x 11 in sheet of paper will make a large two-panel or smallish French-fold card. It can, of course, be cut to any shape but you may have to sacrifice the attractive deckle edge. You can make large sheets, say for wrapping paper, by dipping the mold without the deckle (which will give thinner edges) and placing the sheets on a large couching cloth so that they overlap.

Paper left to dry naturally will have a coarse texture. If you prefer a smooth finish, try pressing it between glass or laminated plastic while it is still moist. Another method is simply to iron each sheet dry after pressing.

There are, as you can see, many possible variations to make each sheet of paper quite different. For those prepared to experiment, papermaking offers endless delights and discoveries.

5 Lettering ❖ ❖ ❖ ❖ ❖ ❖ ❖ ❖ ❖ ❖ ❖ ❖ ❖ ❖

Beautiful lettering can be a feature of a card and can convey your message of thanks or concern in a way that a design cannot. However, all finished greeting cards carry some lettering - if not on the front, then on the inside. If you have spent time and thought designing and making a card, it would seem a pity to spoil it with a message hastily scrawled. This chapter covers the basics of good lettering so that your message won't shame the card that carries it.

Materials

The shape and sharpness of your letters will be determined by the type of pen you select. A fine ball-point pen can give you neat lettering but the result may lack presence. On the other hand, lettering in a thick felt pen or marker can look clumsy. Of these single-tipped pens, I prefer a fine-to-medium marker.

More interesting lettering can be gained by using a square-ended implement, such as a nib, and ink. Nibs come in different widths and can be cut at different angles for left-handers or right-handers. You also have a choice between a dip pen (a metal nib in a pen holder) and a pen with an inbuilt reservoir for ink. Dip pens giver the writer greater control, but are harder to master. If you are new to the craft of calligraphy or lettering, you might invest in an inexpensive introductory set with several nibs and an integrated pen unit. With such a nib, use a non-waterproof black ink, though you might like to experiment with colored inks after some practice.

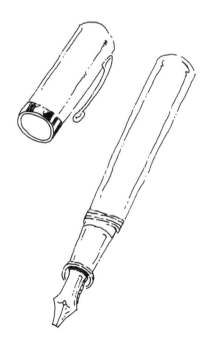

Different types of paper and card will react quite differently to ink. If the paper has too much size, or coating, the ink will be repelled; too little size (or none in the case of blotting paper) and the ink will spread through the fibres. Test the reaction to ink on a scrap before you start writing on a finished greeting card. You will also need a clean sheet of paper or thin card on which to rest your hand and guard your work from being smudged.

Once you have discovered the principles of good lettering, consider using materials other than pen and ink to write on the front of a card. Lettering can be painted, embroidered, embossed, and even quilled!

An integrated calligraphy pen

Forming letters

The principles of using a calligraphy pen can be learned in a very simple way. Bind two pencils together with a piece of tape at each end and then, holding them at a comfortable angle but making sure both leads touch the paper, form large letters. If you shave some of the wood from the side of each pencil, the lines they draw will be closer together. The broad-edged nib on a calligraphy pen produces the same thick and thin lines if held at a constant angle.

A double pencil produces the effect of a broad-edged nib

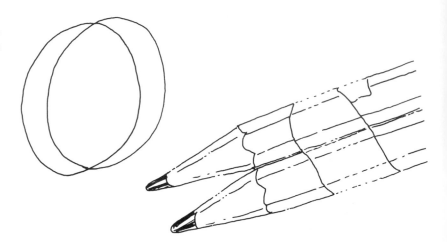

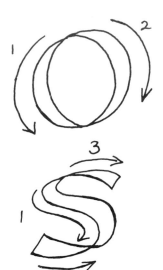

Form letters in several strokes

When using such a pen, the formation of each letter is dictated by the arrangement of thick and thin lines. Broad pen strokes should be pulled towards you, so the letter **O** is usually formed in two strokes, each starting at the top. The letter **S**, on the other hand, is most often formed in three strokes.

There are many traditional scripts, such as Roman, Italic, Gothic and Uncials, in which the letters have shared characteristics; for example Uncial letters tend to be wide, with thick vertical strokes, while Italics incline to the right. Whether you learn to copy such a script or develop your own style is up to you, but you should try to form letters that look as though they belong together.

The "weight" of each letter is determined by its height and the width of the nib used. In the diagram to the left, each black square represents a nib width; this ladder is made with the nib turned to produce the widest stroke. As a rough guide, a good weight is achieved if a lower case letter is four or five times the height of your pen stroke. However, a difference in proportion is one of the features which distinguishes one style of lettering from another. This notion of weight, and the suggestions which follow, apply no matter what type of writing implement you are using.

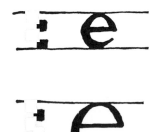

Varying the weight of a letter

Spacing

To keep your lettering straight and a constant weight, it is a very good idea to rule up some pencil lines as a guide. The most important lines are the base line and the x-line, but an ascender and descender line are useful for the beginner. First, try out a few different sizes of letter to see what looks best for your nib width. Rule up your base line and x-line, then add the other lines in proportion (the diagram gives you a suggested ratio). These pencil lines should be carefully erased when you have finished.

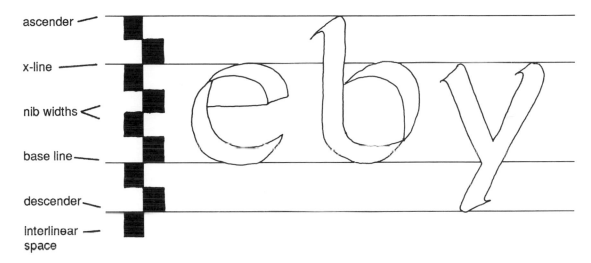

ascender

x-line

nib widths

base line

descender

interlinear space

Guide lines for vertical spacing

The distance between letters should vary according to their shape. For example, the greatest space should lie between two straight-sided letters such as **I** and **R**, while curved and angled letters such as **D** and **A** should nearly overlap. To see the effect, look at the different spacing of the word **BIRTHDAY**. Words should be spaced so they have room to breathe.

BIRTHDAY

BIRTHDAY

Adjusting horizontal spacing

When writing a long message, think of the best place to break a line - try it out on a scrap of paper first before writing it neatly. The best line breaks will be those that both improve readability and please the eye. Choose whether you want the message centered, staggered, or aligned to the left. If you wish to center it, you will need to write a draft and measure the length of each line, to calculate how and where each line should start.

Different ways of arranging your
message

Centered

> Dear Jem
> Wishing you a great day
> As you celebrate your 21st
> Love Kirsty

Staggered

> Our congratulations
> On your graduation
> From the Knox family

Aligned

> Dear Karl
> May this Christmas season
> Bring you much joy
> And a great year ahead.
> Regards, Kim

The message

If you want to make lettering a feature of your card, you have many options available. You might consider writing the receiver's name or the occasion you are celebrating. A newborn baby's photograph framed with name and date of birth makes a lovely card for friends and relatives. Give your festive greetings an international flavor by writing your message in different languages. Shape your message to form a suitable graphic: a bell, say, for Christmas, or a ship to wish someone Bon Voyage. The possibilities are endless. To get you started, here are two suggested projects for decorating the front of cards.

Double thanks

This project will serve as good preparation for using a calligraphy nib. You can, of course, write a message of your own choosing.

❖ Cut and score a two-panel card measuring 7 x 4½ in using light colored card or paper.
❖ Rule a line 1¼ in from the fold, and another one 2⅜ in from the fold; these will be your x-lines.
❖ Rule lines at 2 in and 3⅛ in; these will be your base lines.
❖ Rule lines at 1 in and 3½ in from the fold; these are your ascender and descender lines.
❖ Using a sharp knife, carefully pare the wood along one edge of the two pencils and tape them together at both ends.
❖ Hold the pencils at an angle and make smooth strokes.
❖ Run over the pencil lines with a fine-tipped felt pen.
❖ Draw a border ¼ in from the edges of the card.

You will need:
  light-colored card
  a ruler
  two HB pencils
  a knife
  sticky tape
  a fine-tipped felt pen

True-love knot

You will need:
   2 sheets white paper
   a pencil
   tracing paper
   a fine-nibbed pen
   ink
   colored card
   double-sided tape

This endless ribbon of poem comes from a 17th century English valentine. While it looks difficult, it is simply a case of careful spacing and a steady hand. Don't copy the shape of the letters; use whatever style you find most comfortable so that letters don't distract you from fitting the words in the space available. If you don't have a calligraphy pen, use a medium-tipped felt pen.

❖ Practice some strokes with your pen until comfortable with it.
❖ If your paper is not too opaque, place it over the pattern and pen the outline of the love knot, trying to pause only at the junction of two lines. If you cannot see the pattern through the paper, use tracing paper and pencil to transfer the outline onto your paper.
❖ Place a clean sheet of paper to half cover the knot so you can rest your hand without smudging your work.
❖ Fill the knot with the poem printed below (or one of your own), keeping the guard sheet in the same position and turning the love knot around as needed.
❖ Cut and score a three-panel mount with a front measuring 8½ x 5¾ in and a window measuring 7 x 4¼ in and mount love knot with double-sided tape (see pages 11-13).

TRUE love is a precious pleasure
Rich delight, unvalued treasure
Two firm hearts in one heart meeting
Clasping hand in hand, ne'er fleeting
Wreathlike, like a maze entwining
Two fair minds in one combining
Foe to faithless vows perfidious
True love is a knot religious
Dead to the sins that flaming rise
Through beauty's soul-seducing eyes
Deaf to gold enchanting witches
Love for virtue not for riches
Such is true love's boundless measure
True love is a precious pleasure.

6 Cut-outs ❖ ❖ ❖ ❖ ❖ ❖ ❖ ❖ ❖ ❖ ❖ ❖ ❖ ❖

As well as being attracted by colorful and aesthetic designs, everyone is fascinated by cards that have depth of perspective. A folded card has inherent potential and this section suggests some ideas which take advantage of that extra dimension. You can adapt any of these to the occasion you are celebrating. The idea behind the Advent card, for example, could produce a family tree for a wedding, or a card marking the milestones of a person's life up to a special birthday.

On a practical level, all the designs require careful cutting, including some free-hand. Make sure the blade on your knife is sharp. Cut some practice curves and lines on scrap card first.

One piece of advice: if you have made a cut-through card, take care where you write your message on the inside panel so that it doesn't spoil the effect of your work.

Window box

❖ Score and fold card to make a 5 x 7 in portrait.
❖ Draw the pattern for the window casement on tracing paper, turn the paper around and draw a matching casement, then transfer this onto the inside of the card's front panel.
❖ Carefully cut along the lines.
❖ Still on the inside, score the edge of the casements so that they open outwards.
❖ Cut the pieces of the scene from colored card and glue them on the inside of the other panel so that they are visible through the open window. Make sure the hill extends below the window and does not "float" in mid-air.

You will need:
  scraps of colored card
  pencil & ruler
  tracing paper
  glue
  a craft knife
  white card

Elements in the scene

Pattern for window casement

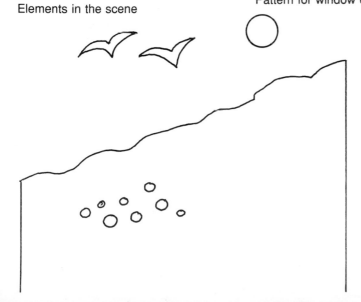

Stained glass

You will need:
clear plastic
permanent marker pens
white paper
black card
a pencil
a ruler
a craft knife
double-sided tape

The window in this mount has been cut to look like the lead between pieces of stained glass. I have used permanent marking pens to color a piece of clear plastic (sold for covering books) but you could use some pre-colored cellophane to achieve the same effect.

❖ Measure and cut a two- or three-panel mount to make a 4½ x 6 in portrait shape.
❖ Transfer the pattern onto the inside of the front or middle panel in pencil.
❖ Use a craft knife to cut out the flower and its leaves, being careful not to cut the strips between them. If you do slip, cut a strip of sticky tape and attach it to the inside.
❖ Place plastic over the pattern and hold it in place with removable tape.
❖ Use marker pens to fill in, and extend beyond, marked areas.
❖ Put the plastic behind the window and check that no gaps will show, then stick it in place with tape.
❖ Cut a piece of white paper or card, slightly larger than the window, then stick it behind the plastic.
❖ Seal both the plastic and paper into the mount with double-sided tape.

Pattern for stained glass

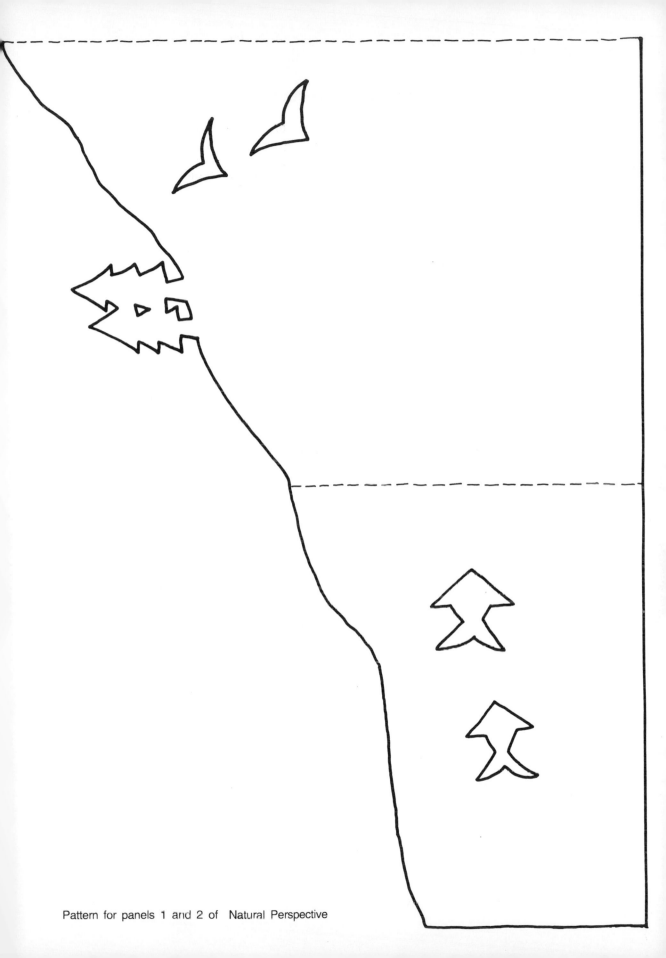

Pattern for panels 1 and 2 of Natural Perspective

Natural perspective

You will need:
green card
blue card
a ruler
a craft knife
glue
a pencil

This card makes use of two colors and a concertina fold to give a simple design some depth.

❖ Cut a 15 x 6½ in piece of green card and then a matching piece of blue.
❖ Spread glue on the whole surface of one piece and stick the two together.
❖ On the blue side, measure 5 in along the long edge and score a line to mark off a third of the card, then gently fold.
❖ Turn over to the green side, measure 5 in from the other end score and fold.
❖ Transfer the pattern onto the blue side in pencil. Note that the pattern covers the first two panels only; the third is uncut.
❖ Making sure the card is unfolded, use a sharp craft knife to cut along the pencilled lines.
❖ Erase any visible pencil lines.

Cut-and-twist figures

You will need:
a pencil
an eraser
a craft knife
stiff colored card

This method of "almost cutting" allows images to stand out from their base. Patterns for all numbers are provided so you can make anybody's age or, say, the number of their wedding anniversary. You can apply the same principle to alphabet letters or any small design to create cards for all occasions.

❖ Score and fold a two-panel card to fit your message.
❖ Sketch your design on the front panel in pencil.
❖ Divide each number or letter in two with a vertical pencil line.
❖ Revise your sketch so that each line crossing this vertical divide is broken by at least ⅛ in. Erase the vertical line.
❖ Use a sharp knife to cut along the revised pencil lines, being careful to leave the gaps at the line breaks.
❖ Erase any visible pencil lines.
❖ Holding the card open, gently twist the figure so it juts forward and backward from the body of the card.

Patterns for Cut-and-twist numbers

Motifs for the Advent card

Advent card

You will need:
scraps of colored card
or paper
two 7¾ x 11½ in sheets
of white paper
24 x 16 in red card
a pencil
a ruler
an eraser
a craft knife
glue

Advent calendars and cards are traditionally given at the end of November to count the days down to Christmas. A 24-window card will take a long time to make, though you can be sure it will be fully appreciated! If you wish to make fewer windows, say 12, simply adjust the measurements and choose the symbols you prefer.

❖ Rule pencil lines dividing the red card into four quarters, then score to make a French fold (see page 9).
❖ On the front of the card, rule the grid in pencil.
❖ Draw the numbers 1 to 24 in pencil in the appropriate boxes, unfold the card and then use a craft knife to carefully cut out the numbers.
❖ Cut two pieces of white paper or card, each measuring 7¾ x 11½ in.
❖ Apply glue to the back of the numbered panel at various points and stick down one of the pieces of white card.
❖ Using your craft knife, cut three edges of each window, then score the fourth edge on the inside so that the window opens outwards.
❖ Glue the other piece of white card in place, so that it can be seen through the windows.
❖ Using scissors or a craft knife, cut the motifs (shown on the previous page) from brightly colored card or paper.
❖ Glue the motifs onto the white paper so that each one appears in a separate window.
❖ Close the windows and press the folded card between heavy books so that, when the card is given, the windows will lie closed until pried open.

Score one edge of each box and cut the other three

Grid for the front panel

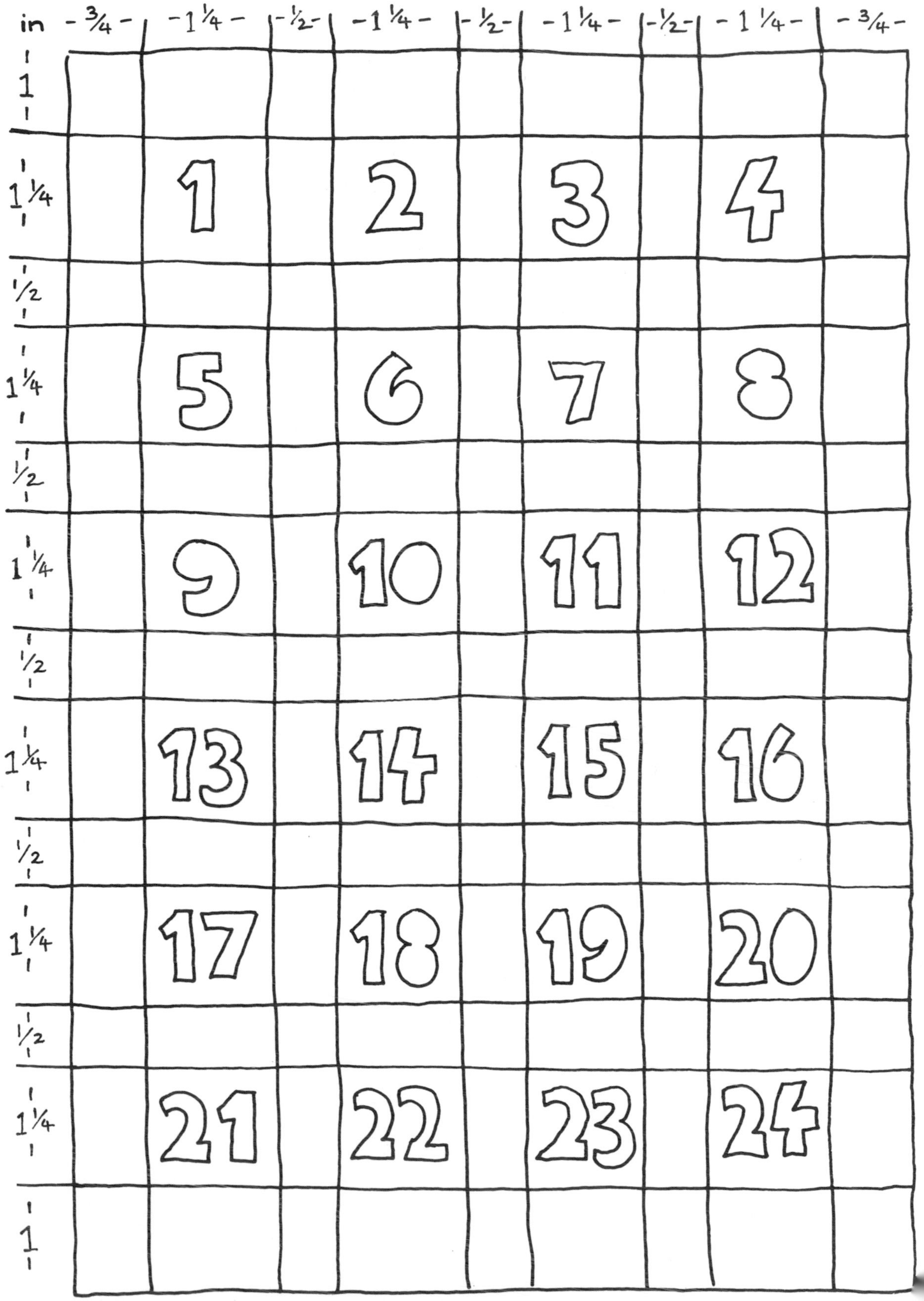

in	− ¾ −	− 1¼ −	− ½ −	− 1¼ −	− ½ −	− 1¼ −	− ½ −	− 1¼ −	− ¾ −
1									
1¼		1		2		3		4	
½									
1¼		5		6		7		8	
½									
1¼		9		10		11		12	
½									
1¼		13		14		15		16	
½									
1¼		17		18		19		20	
½									
1¼		21		22		23		24	
1									

7 Paper Appliqué ❖❖❖❖❖❖❖❖❖❖

Gluing down bits of paper seems a simple occupation but the number of names given to it shows just how popular a pastime it is. Variations on the theme include collage, découpage and déchirage, which come from the French words for gluing, cutting and tearing. This chapter looks at a few such ways of decorating cards which can be clumped togther under the name paper appliqué - French once again - simply meaning applied.

Traditional approaches

Découpage developed in France during the eighteenth century when the women of the court cut up engravings and painted varnish over them to imitate the hand-painted lacquerwork of Chinese furniture. The development of printing, and in particular color printing, meant that pictures on paper were more readily available and découpage became a middle-class pursuit which was especially popular in England. Printers fed the craze by producing colorful pre-cut images known as scraps.

The Victorians made a hobby of sticking these sentimental pictures on screens, boxes and many other objects. More often, they stuck them, unlaquered, in scrapbooks (which were highly valued as gifts) or on ornate cards. This, indeed, was the period that saw Valentines and other greeting cards become part of our culture.

Recently, there has been a renewed interest in Victoriana and you may find scraps commercially available. It is more fun, however, to search for your own scraps amongst gift wrapping, expired calendars and diaries, remaindered art books and other printed material. Rather than throwing away old greeting cards, cut out any pictures that interest you and reuse them in a different way. Keep pictures untrimmed until you wish to use them, as they are less likely to get damaged that way.

Paper doilies can be used to make very attractive and delicate cards. Depending on the style and size available, you might trim several small motifs from the border, or remove the center piece and use the border whole. Mount on a dark card to create a contrast and show up the detail of the doily.

Raised découpage

You will need:
> *printed scraps*
> *small scissors*
> *a craft knife*
> *sticky tape*
> *colored card*

The scraps you select will probably set the tone of your card, but you can add something extra by giving the picture depth. The easiest way is to stick pictures down with a double-sided tape made of foam but the following instructions offer a substitute.

❖ Find a printed scene that can be segmented or a number of prints that can be combined.
❖ Hold the print in your left hand and the scissors in your right (or vice versa if you are left-handed).
❖ Trim off the background of the picture, turning the print as you feed the paper into the blades. Do not move the scissors around the print.
❖ Trim delicate areas with a craft knife.
❖ On a spare sheet of paper, arrange parts of the picture so they overlap.
❖ Measure and cut a two-panel card to fit the picture.
❖ Make a cushion of tape for each part of the picture: cut 2 in of sticky tape, and fold it inwards so that it is adhesive on both sides and slightly padded.
❖ Build up the picture, starting from the back and sticking picture on picture to get a three-dimensional effect.

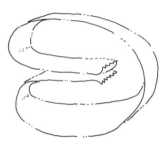

Making a pillow of tape

Wildflower collages

You will need:
> *a pencil*
> *tracing paper*
> *a craft knife*
> *a thick black felt pen*
> *glue*
> *red card*
> *light green card*
> *dark green card*

Using printed paper as an appliqué gives you a ready-made picture as the focus of your card. If you choose undecorated paper, you will need to create a picture or pattern yourself. These bold designs feature two Australian flowers: Kangaroo Paw and Sturt's Desert Pea. Their form and colors make them striking alternatives to the usual holly seen on most Christmas cards.

❖ Cut and score a two-panel card with a front panel measurement of 6½ x 5 in.
❖ Transfer the pattern pieces onto card of the appropriate color.
❖ Cut along the heavy lines with a craft knife.
❖ Assemble the pieces of the flower on the card and glue in position.
❖ Outline the shapes with a black felt pen.
❖ Draw in the black boss on the Sturt's Desert Peas as well as the lines dividing the petals and leaves.

Note that the Desert Pea design suits an upright card with a side fold, while the Kangaroo Paw fits a card with the fold at the top.

Déchirage squares, Laminated shapes and Tissue lambs (page 52)

Déchirage squares

You will need:
        a pencil
        a ruler
        glue
        colored tissue paper
        white card

Paper which has been torn has a softer appearance than that which has been cut. Tissue paper is particularly easy to tear and is available in a great range of colors.

❖ Cut and score a two-panel card with a front panel measuring 5¼ x 5¼ in.
❖ Make a series of pencil marks 1½ in apart along one edge of a sheet of tissue.
❖ Hold the bulk of the sheet down with a ruler and tear 1½ in strips by pulling the corner towards you.
❖ Tear each strip into 1½ in squares, again using the ruler.
❖ Spread glue very thinly on the tissue squares and arrange them on the card in a checkerboard fashion with a narrow gutter between them.
❖ Press by placing a clean sheet of paper on top and smoothing down with the side of your hand.

Laminated shapes

You will need:
        colored tissue paper
        a craft knife
        self-adhesive plastic
        cream card

As tissue paper is very delicate, a covering of clear self-adhesive plastic can protect your card and add to its life-span. It can also make gluing unnecessary, as it holds the torn shapes securely in place. This material is sold in rolls for covering books and is available from most stationery stores.

❖ Cut and score a two-panel card of any size.
❖ Tear scraps from various colors of tissue paper and arrange them on the card.
❖ Cut a piece of adhesive plastic ½ in larger than the front panel of your card.
❖ Peel off the backing paper and carefully lower the plastic, sticky side down, onto the card.
❖ Use the side of your hand to smooth out any pockets of air.
❖ Turn the card over and trim the excess plastic close to the edges of the card.

Tissue lambs

You will need:
        a pencil
        a ruler
        glue
        a silver felt pen
        white, black & green
              tissue paper
        blue card

This slightly frivolous card would bring a smile to the lips of most people, but its texture will definitely appeal to a child celebrating a second birthday. For older toddlers, you could extend the width of the panel and add some extra sheep.

❖ Cut and score a two-panel card in blue, with a front panel which measures 7 x 4½ in.

- Draw the body of the sheep on the card.
- Place a sheet of black tissue over the pattern for the sheep and use a sharp pencil to draw around the head and legs.
- Using both hands, gently tear the tissue around the pencil lines; the fibres should be weakened so the shape is easier to tear.
- Glue the legs and head in place on the card.
- Tear squares of white and black tissue paper, roughly 1 in square, and scrunch them into balls.
- Spread glue on the card before sticking tissue balls on to form one white body and one black body.
- Dot the eyes in with a silver felt pen.
- Tear a strip of green tissue paper 8 x 1 in.
- Fold the long edges in towards the middle and twist gently.
- Glue on the card to form a small hill.
- Add some clumps of grass by twisting short strips of green tissue and gluing them in place.

Rolling tissue into strips

Satin checkerboard card

8 Weaving ❖❖❖❖❖❖❖❖❖❖❖❖❖❖❖❖

We normally think of weaving as a means of making fabric for clothing or furnishings, but it has other possibilities: you can weave strips of paper, ribbon or other material into a panel for an attractive card. The design can be a simple checkerboard of color or a more complex motif: either way, the interlacing pattern is sure to catch everyone's eye.

When planning your card, work out how many slits are needed to keep ends hidden from the front of the card. Make the slits long enough to thread strips through, but narrow enough to hold them in place.

Satin checkerboard

This is a good card to use up any oddments of fabric you might have; for the card shown, I have used strips of a polyester material that resembles satin. Don't worry if the fabric frays a little, but avoid overhandling.

You will need:
  colored fabrics
  pencil
  ruler
  craft knife
  black card

❖ Cut the fabric into strips ½ in wide and at least 6 in long.
❖ Cut and score the black card into a three panel base with a front panel measurement of 5½ x 7 in (see page 11).
❖ On the inside of the center panel, rule a horizontal pencil line 1 in from the top and another the same distance from the bottom. Leave a ¾ in margin at either end and mark a series of dots ⅜ in apart along the lines.
❖ Cut vertical slots to join the parallel dots; this should give you eleven slots.
❖ With the front of the card facing you, thread one end of a fabric strip through the first slot and down through the second slot, up through the third and so on until the tenth slot.
❖ Ignore the last slot, keeping the end of the strip at the back of the card. Pull the strip carefully until there are equal lengths at either end. Push the woven strip to the bottom of the panel.
❖ Thread the next strip through the second slot and continue as above, though this time you will need the last slot to bring the fabric to the back. Push the strip down.
❖ Weave the next strip through the first slot and continue as above.
❖ Continue weaving the strips, pushing them down so that they bunch slightly, until no more will fit.
❖ Make sure they are evenly spread, trim the ends to ½ in beyond the first and last slots, and glue them down to the back of the middle panel.
❖ Run a line of glue around the perimeter of the middle panel and glue down the backing panel.

Pierced heart

You will need:
  pencil
  eraser
  tracing paper
  scissors
  craft knife
  glue
  red card
  cream card

This one cheats a little - what looks like a single woven arrow is actually two pieces with a hidden join - but it would make a dramatic statement on Valentine's Day. It will probably require a handmade envelope because of its unusual shape.

❖ Cut and score red card to make a two-panel base with a front measuring 6 x 6 in.
❖ Use the tracing paper to transfer the heart pattern onto your base; the broken line should be aligned with the folded edge.
❖ Use scissors to cut out your card base. Be careful not to cut along the broken line or the back panel will become detached.
❖ Unfold the card base and use a craft knife to cut the slots marked on the pattern.
❖ Use tracing paper to transfer the arrow pattern onto cream card and cut out the parts.
❖ From the right of the heart, weave the shaft of the arrow head through three slots, so that the arrow head lies on top of the heart and the end is hidden on the inside of the card.
❖ From the left, weave the shaft of the arrow tail through three slots, as above. The tail should be positioned so that the card will stand without any support.
❖ Open the card and position the two halves of the arrow so they overlap, then glue the overlapping sections together.
(This can be done so that the joins are hidden on both sides.)

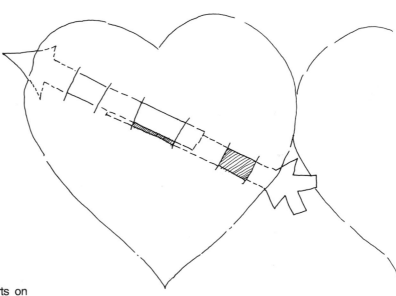

Join the arrow parts on
the inside of the card

Pattern for the Pierced heart card

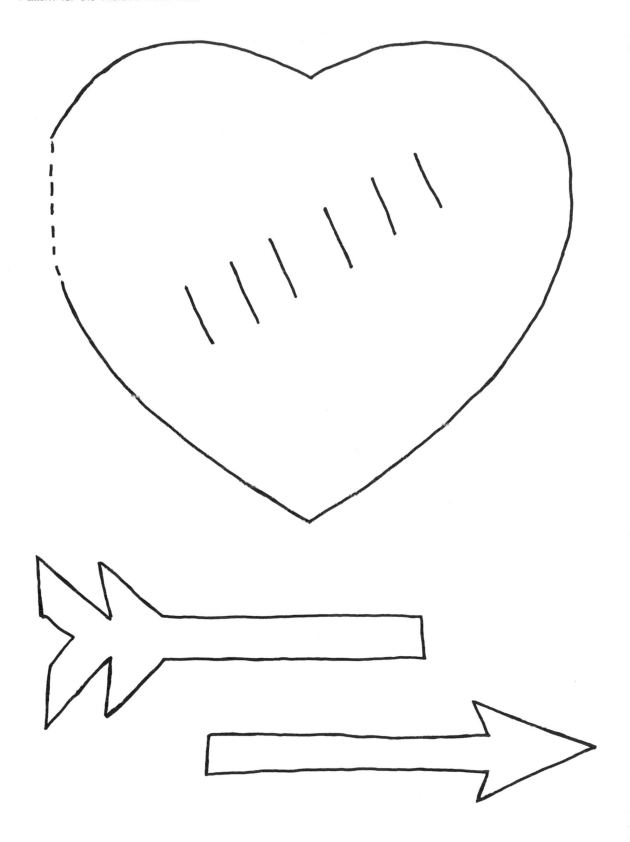

Pierced heart (page 56) and Ribbon weave (page 60)

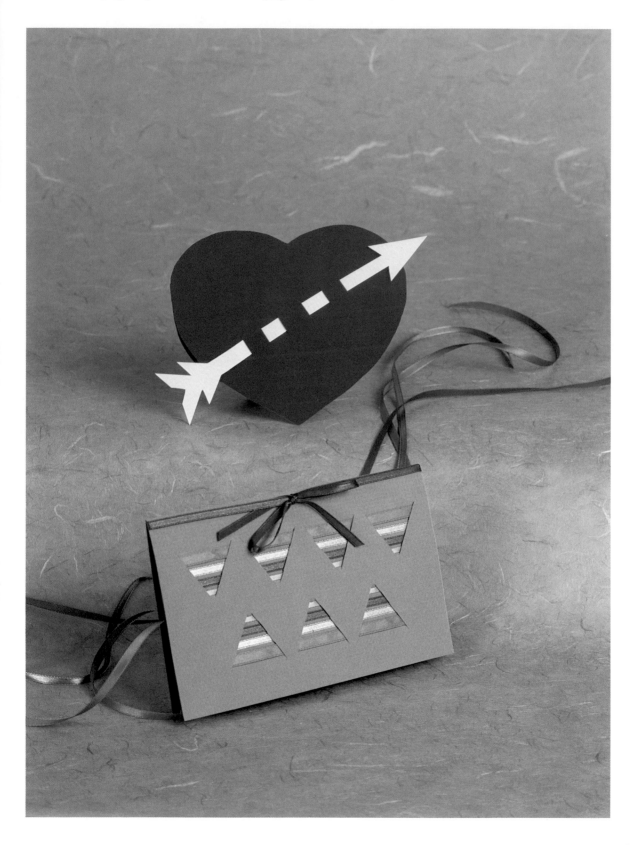

Ribbon weave

You will need:
- 12-in-lengths of satin ribbon
- scissors
- pencil
- ruler
- eraser
- craft knife
- glue
- colored card

Ribbons are available from sewing departments or craft shops in a range of lovely colors, widths and textures. Keep a supply of them, as they can be used to trim plainer cards. This example uses scraps of satin ribbons between ¼ and ½ in wide.

❖ Score and fold the card into a 6½ x 4 in two-panel base.
❖ On an inside panel, rule 2 pairs of parallel pencil lines; the distance between the lines of each pair should be no more than a sixteenth of an inch wider than the total width of your ribbons.
❖ Draw the angled lines shown in the diagram and then slit the card along these lines, being careful not to cut further than indicated.
❖ Erase the pencil lines.
❖ Weave each ribbon through the slots so that it starts and ends on the inside of the card.
❖ Trim the ribbon ends and glue them in place.
❖ For a finishing touch, tie an extra ribbon around the fold so that it sits along the spine.

Pattern for ribbon weave card

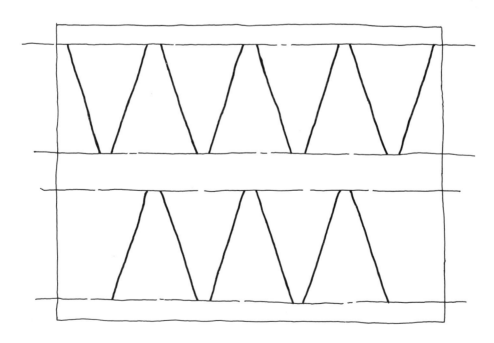

Christmas tree

This delicate design needs quite a bit of patience. I discovered one Christmas that it wasn't ideal for mass production but everyone who received it appreciated the effort. Try it and see!

❖ Cut a strip of brown paper ½ in wide.
❖ Cut strips of light and dark green paper with varying widths, between ⅛ and ¼ in.
❖ Cut a 1½ x 2½ in rectangle from the paper you will use as your card base.
❖ Being careful not to cut the top or bottom of the rectangle, use your knife to cut the slots shown in the diagram.
❖ Weave a dark strip so that it appears only between the two middle slots. Push the strip up so it forms the tip of the tree.
❖ Weave a light strip so that it appears twice, once on each side of the first strip. Push it gently to the top.
❖ Continue weaving, alternating dark and light strips, until 6 strips have been used. Use strips of varying width to add interest and, when you reach the last strip, select one that will fit neatly in the space that remains.
❖ Weave the brown strip through the two middle slots, to form the trunk of the tree.
❖ Trim the edges of the strips, cutting at an angle.
❖ Cut card 7 x 8 in, then score and fold to form a 7 x 4 in two panel base.
❖ On the back of the woven tree, dab a little glue on several points, including the cross bars - this will keep all the woven strips in place.
❖ Glue the woven tree in the center of your card base.

You will need:
light green paper
dark green paper
dark brown paper
ruler
craft knife
cutting board
glue
thin cream card
*   or stiff paper*

Pattern of slots for tree

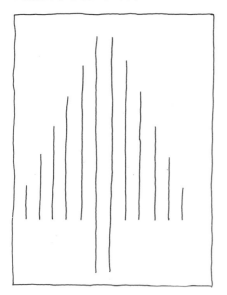

Weaving the strips

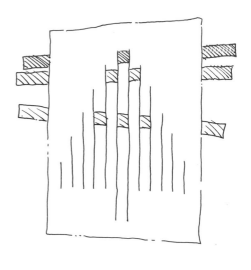

Starburst (page 64), Pop-up swan (page 65) and Sculpted flowers

9 Paper Sculpture ❖❖❖❖❖❖❖❖❖❖❖

Paper comes to us in a flat form but, with a few tricks, it can be molded into unusual and beautiful shapes. Choose a firm paper that will hold a shape well and make sure you get a crisp result by keeping your hands clean and your workspace clear.

Sculpted flowers

The technique of scoring has more uses than folding the panels of a card. By scoring curved lines and easing the fold with fingertips, you can create lovely flowing shapes. This raised card would get squashed in an envelope, so make a box or give it by hand.

❖ Using tracing paper and pencil, transfer the pattern onto white paper to mark out three flowers and leaves.

❖ Cut the star at the center of each flower, taking care not to drag the paper.

❖ Holding the craft-knife like a pen, lightly score along the dotted lines, then cut along the heavy lines.

❖ Take a flower and, with the scored side on the bottom, push a skewer through the star to form stamens.

❖ Holding the flower on the skewer, gently pinch each petal so that it folds upwards.

❖ Hold a leaf in both hands and pinch along the fold, allowing it to curve as scored. Sculpt all the flowers and leaves as above.

❖ Cut and score a two-panel card with a front panel measurement of 5½ x 5½ in.

❖ Use the skewer to apply small amounts of glue to the back of the flowers and stick them on the card, being careful not to flatten the stamens.

❖ Apply glue to the stems of the leaves and tuck them under the flowers so that the scored curve is raised.

You will need:
a pencil
tracing paper
a craft knife
a skewer
glue
strong white paper
green card

Pattern for flower and leaf

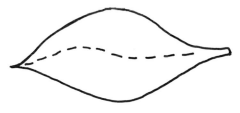

Use your fingertips to press the pieces into shape

Starburst

You will need:
  a pencil
  tracing paper
  a ruler
  a craft knife
  glue
  white paper
  red card

If, as a child, you ever made chains of paper dolls, you will already be familiar with the principles behind this card. A star on red card will make a stunning Christmas greeting but the idea can be adapted to any motif as long as it has an edge that can be folded.

❖ Cut a 12 x 6 in piece of white paper.
❖ Mark dots along both of the long edges at 2 in intervals.
❖ Using your fingertips, fold on alternate sides to make a concertina fold, as shown in the diagram.

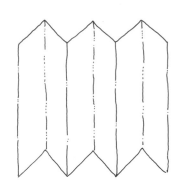

Note the fold lines in the pattern

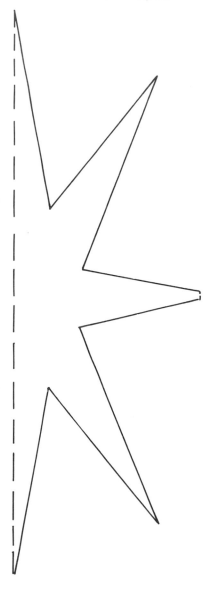

❖ Transfer the pattern onto the paper concertina so that the center point of the star touches the folded edge.
❖ Cut through all the layers with a knife. Only cut along the heavy lines; leave a connecting tip on the center point.
❖ Put a dab of glue between the second and third panel, and another between the fourth and fifth, so that the body of the star holds together but the points are still separate.
❖ Cut and score a two-panel card in red, with a front panel measurement of 6 x 4½ in.
❖ Position the long edge of the star along the card's inside fold and stick it in place with a dab of glue on each of the sides.
❖ On another piece of paper, draw a complete star by tracing one half then reversing the tracing paper to draw the other half.
❖ Cut out this star and glue it on the front of your card.

Pop-up swan

Pop-up cards are always an immediate success with children and adults alike. This design suggests the elegance that can be achieved; if you are trying to please a child, you might consider changing the swan to a farmyard or zoo animal. When designing your own, make sure the figure does not extend beyond the limits of your folded card.

You will need:
  a pencil
  tracing paper
  a ruler
  a craft knife
  an eraser
  glue
  blue card
  a large sheet of white paper

❖ Cut and score a two-panel card in blue, with a front panel measurement of 7 x 5 in.
❖ Cut a piece of white paper to measure 16 x 6 in, then score and fold in half to measure 8 x 6 in.
❖ Using tracing paper and pencil, transfer the swan pattern onto the paper so that the broken line at the top of the wing lies along the fold. Note that the other end should extend right down to the bottom of your paper.

Shortened pattern for swan

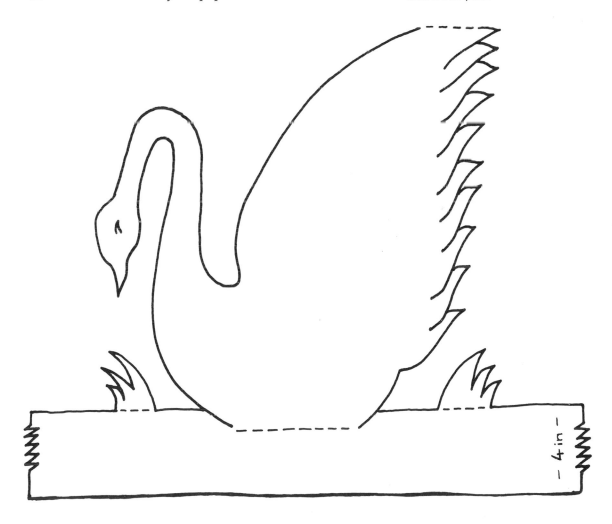

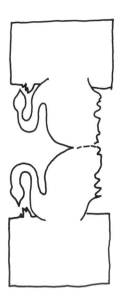

The full cut-out

❖ Use a craft knife to cut through the two layers of paper at the same time. Cut only along the heavy lines and, when you reach the tail feathers, start each cut from the body of the swan and cut towards the feather tip.
❖ Carefully erase any pencil marks left on the swan.
❖ Unfold the cut-out and use your fingertips to fold along the base of the swan and the rushes so that they stand up.
❖ Fold the eye down on the inside and glue together the two sides of the head, back to the top of the curved neck.
❖ Open the blue card and position the white cut-out on the inside so the rectangles are 1 in apart and the swan stands up.
❖ Hold in place with a dab of glue and close the card to test that no white paper peeps out, and that the swan folds neatly. If necessary, reposition the cut-out or trim the white rectangles.
❖ Open the card and glue the rectangles firmly in place.
❖ Decorate the front of the card with some white rushes, or with a neatly written message.

Clear impressions

You will need:
   dried rice
   string
   glue
   white cardboard
   thick paper
   a hand-towel
   newspaper
   large books

Impressing and embossing are two ways of making a raised image on paper. In both methods, the fibres of the paper are stretched to take on a new shape either by pressing objects into the paper (impressing) or by pressing the paper into a mold (embossing).

Thick handmade paper is particularly suitable for these projects; indeed, the process of impressing can be added as a stage of papermaking, as described in Chapter 4. In this project, the design is made into a permanent block which can be used to impress a number of sheets.

❖ Cut a piece of cardboard 4½ x 8½ in.
❖ Arrange grains of rice in the shape of heads of wheat and glue on the card.
❖ Cut pieces of string to represent the stems and leaf and glue them in place.
❖ Place this "block" on a folded newspaper, slightly to one side.
❖ Cut a 8½ x 8 in piece from thick, attractive paper.
❖ Dip it briefly in a basin of water.
❖ Lay the paper down with the right-hand-half covering the block so that when the card is folded the design will appear on the front.
❖ Cover this with a small towel and smooth out any creases.
❖ Stack a pile of books on top and leave for several hours.
❖ Remove the books and towel, and carefully peel the paper off the block.
❖ When the paper is quite dry, score in half to form a two-panel card.

Make a block from rice and string

Embossed letters

You will need:
> tracing paper
> a pencil
> 8 x 5 in linoleum
> lino-cutters
> a toothbrush
> a burnisher
> light-coloured card

The beauty of an embossed card comes from the play of light and shadow across the design and for this to be clearly visible you will need to use a light-colored card. Thicker paper or card is a little more difficult to emboss but gives a better impression. You will get the most pleasing result if the linoleum is cut with sharp lines and smooth hollows. Lino-cutters are available in inexpensive sets from craft shops. A burnisher is a specially shaped metal tool. If you can't buy one from an art or craft supply shop, substitute any metal implement which has a smooth rounded point.

Letters are an especially good subject for this treatment because they have well-defined shapes and features. You might like to emboss someone's name for a birthday card, or a message of good luck or thanks. If you create a picture design, keep it simple.

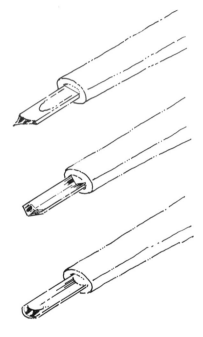

Straight, V- and U-shaped blades

❖ Cut a two-panel card with a front panel measuring 8¼ x 5 in.
❖ Trace the pattern onto the tracing paper in pencil.
❖ Lay the tracing on the linoleum with pencil-work down, so that when you scribble in pencil over them, the reversed design will appear on the linoleum.
❖ Warm the linoleum slightly by placing it in the sun or in a very low oven: this will make it easier to cut.
❖ Use a straight-edged blade to cut along the lines of the letters.
❖ Cut at an angle, sloping towards the center of the letter.
❖ Use a V-shaped blade to gouge the linoleum from the letters, pushing the cutter away from your body.
❖ Use a U-shaped blade to smooth out the hollows of the letters.
❖ Brush the finished lino-cut with an old toothbrush to clean away loose fragments.
❖ Erase any remaining pencil marks from the lino-cut.
❖ Run the tip of the burnisher along the hollows to ensure they are quite smooth.
❖ Hold the card briefly over a steaming kettle; this will dampen the fibres and allow them to stretch.
❖ Open the card and position it on the lino-cut so that the front panel lies face down on the design.
❖ Use the flat foot of the burnisher to establish the outline of the letters.
❖ Use the toe of the burnisher to gently impress the hollows of the letters. If you press too hard, the paper may tear.
❖ When all parts of the design are evenly impressed, lift the card and check your work. If necessary, the card can be carefully positioned back on the lino-cut for further burnishing, but if not aligned properly you will blur your original lines.

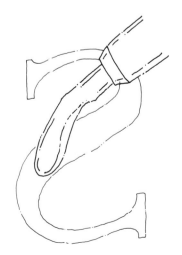

Press the paper into the lino-cut with a burnisher

Trace this pattern onto the linoleum so it is reversed

Paste painting cards (for pattern of window mount see page 12)

10 Painting ❖ ❖ ❖ ❖ ❖ ❖ ❖ ❖ ❖ ❖ ❖ ❖ ❖ ❖ ❖

When I hear the word "painting", I generally think of the full thing: artists with easels and palettes of oils. However, there are plenty of painting methods suitable for people who are not experts with a brush. The free-style approaches described in this chapter allow you to use paint in attractive and fun ways. Once you have set up your work space, the steps are also very quick so you'll find them ideal for making multiple cards as well as matching wrapping paper.

Paste painting

This may look like child's play but, while it is certainly easy and lots of fun, it is no less of a craft for being so. People have used paste to decorate paper since the sixteenth century and the method offers the cardmaker great scope. Wallpaper paste is the easiest to use; if it is not readily available, mix four parts of water to one part of flour, boil while stirring until paste thickens, then leave to cool before adding paint.

❖ Collect suitable implements, such as a sponge, fork, or a comb cut from heavy-duty cardboard.

❖ Using a large bowl, mix wallpaper paste with water in the proportions directed on the packet. Try to prevent lumps developing by sprinkling the powder gently on the water while stirring vigorously. If the paint does become lumpy, you will need to sieve it.

❖ Add paint and stir it in well.

❖ Test the color of your paste mixture on a scrap of card and adjust if required. The color can either darken or lighten slightly when the paste dries.

❖ Lay down plenty of newspaper to cover your work space. Remove each sheet of newspaper as it becomes dirty so that your work doesn't stick or spoil.

❖ Lay your sheet of paper or card on top and use the brush to cover it evenly with paste paint.

❖ Use the implements to make patterns - daubing with a sponge, scraping with a comb and so on. You will need to work quite quickly as the paste will start to dry, especially if spread thinly.

❖ Leave sheets of patterned card to dry. If they curl, wait until they are completely dry and then press between heavy books.

❖ Select sections with good definition and either cut them into two-panel cards or mount them in three-panel cards in a suitable color.

You will need:
  wallpaper paste
  water-based paint
  card or heavy paper
  a bowl
  a mixing spoon
  a wide brush
  patterning tools
  newspaper

Cut a comb from sturdy card

Spattering

You will need:
        acrylic paint
        an old toothbrush
        paint dish
        stiff card or a knife
        paper or card
        newspaper

Here is another technique that can be used in a variety of ways. You can, for example, apply several colors with a toothbrush to achieve a delicate blend of shades, or you can use a large brush and get a bold pattern. The following instructions explain how to use leaves as a mask, preventing the paint from covering the whole area. A word of warning: this can get messy and is best done out of doors.

❖ Select an object with a well-defined and interesting shape.
❖ Cut paper or card into suitable sizes for making two-panel cards.
❖ Thin some acrylic paint with a small amount of water.
❖ Lay plenty of newspaper down, then place your card down with the leaf (or whatever) on top.
❖ Make sure the object lies flat on the card - you may need to weight it with pebbles.
❖ Dip the bristles of the toothbrush in the paint and shake off any excess paint.
❖ Point the head of the brush down at the object and run a piece of stiff card over the bristles towards you.
❖ Dip the brush in paint again when necessary and spatter around the edges of the object, being careful not to drop large splotches of paint onto your work.
❖ Once you have spattered right around the shape, carefully remove the object and leave the card to dry.
❖ Trim as necessary and then score into a two-panel card or mount in a three-panel card.

Pull the scraper towards you so you don't get sprayed by paint

Salt and silk

The beautiful mottled effect gained by sprinkling salt on painted silk can form the basis of a very pleasing card. Rock salt is available from a supermarket, silk paints from an arts and crafts shop. You only need scraps of silk - you may have some offcuts or be able to pick up remnants from a fabric shop. Different salts will give you different patterns but it is impossible to predict what the finished result will be.

❖ Have all the materials ready: you will need to work quickly once the paint is applied.
❖ Lay the silk over the top of an open jar and hold it taut with a rubber band. (A small embroidery frame is a good substitute, though it may get stained.)
❖ Warm some salt in the oven: the dryer the salt, the more moisture it can soak up.
❖ Shake the silk paints before opening, then use a wet brush or eye-dropper to apply paint randomly onto the fabric.
❖ Quickly sprinkle the painted area liberally with salt. Salt attracts moisture and it will randomly soak up some of the pigment from the paint.
❖ Leave everything to dry for an hour, or longer if necessary, and then brush off the salt.
❖ Trim off the unpainted edges of the fabric and cut a rectangle or square.
❖ Use a needle to tease out threads from an edge of the fabric, then carefully pull them to form a fringe. Repeat at each edge of the silk.
❖ Cut and score a two-panel card in a size to suit your piece of patterned silk.
❖ Use double-sided tape to stick the silk square onto the front panel of your card.

Rather than discard the colored salt crystals which this project produces, you might like to glue them onto the front of another two-panel card.

You will need:
  fine white silk
  silk paints
  rock salt
  brush or eye-dropper
  a jar or tin
  a rubber band
  scissors
  a needle
  double-sided tape
  cream card

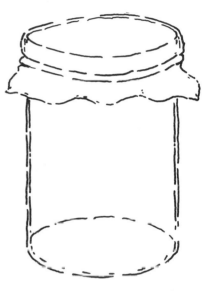

Pull the fabric taut over a jar with an elastic band

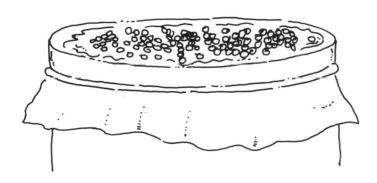

Sprinkle the salt onto the paint while it is still wet

Spatter card (page 72)

Salt and silk card (page 73) and two marbled cards (page 76)

Marbling

You will need:
oil paints
turpentine or white spirit
white paper
a deep foil or plastic tray
jars to mix colors in
paint brushes
toothpicks or skewers
newspaper
colored card
tape or glue

The decorative art of marbling has become popular in recent years and with good reason. The principles can be applied in various ways and even the simplest method, which we will look at here, can give lovely effects.

The characteristic swirled and veined patterns of marbling are achieved by floating colors on liquid and catching them on paper or fabric. Classic marbling techniques require a preparation made from caragheen moss which gives you greater control over the patterns you create. The easiest and cheapest method, however, relies on the fact that oil floats on water.

Note: you will get a better result if you use cheaper, "student" oil paints rather than professional quality ones.

❖ Trim your paper so that it will lie neatly in the tray or dish.
❖ Tear strips of newspaper the same width as the tray.
❖ Fill the tray with water and leave it to stand for ten minutes.
❖ Thin a small amount of oil paint with enough turpentine so that the paint shakes from the brush.

Dropping paint onto the water

❖ Use your brush to flick small droplets of paint on the water. The drops should spread over the surface and form large circles of color. If they drop to the bottom of the tray, add more turpentine to your paint; if they disperse too quickly and disappear, thicken your mixture with more oil paint.

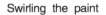

Swirling the paint

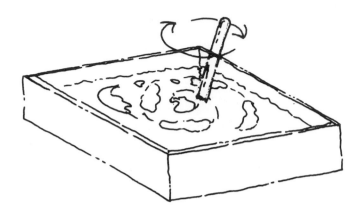

- ❖ Use a stick or other implement to gently swirl the paint.
- ❖ Hold a piece of paper by diagonal corners and lower it so that it lies on the surface of the water. Try to avoid air bubbles as these can spoil the effect.

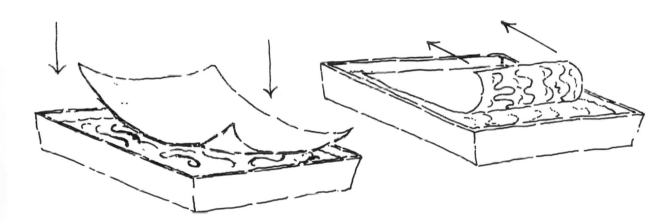

Laying the paper down

Lifting the marbled paper

- ❖ Lift the paper and leave it, pattern upright, on newspaper to dry before ironing flat.
- ❖ To clean remaining specks of paint from the water, skim the surface with a strip of newspaper and start the process again.
- ❖ When you have pressed your marbled paper, cut and score a three-panel mount in a suitable color of card.
- ❖ Cut a window and hold it over the marbling to select the best section. Trim the section and mount it in your card, using double-sided tape or glue (see page 13).

11 Printing ❖❖❖❖❖❖❖❖❖❖❖❖❖❖

In this chapter I've collected various methods of applying ink or paint to cards in a controlled way. Once you have created a design, these methods allow you to make multiple cards with a minimum of effort.

Several of the projects are forms of relief printing, whereby raised sections on a block or object receive ink and so print when pressed on paper. When planning any printing of this type, remember that the printed result will be a mirror image of your block. If printing lettering or a picture with a definite right and left, make sure your block picture is reversed.

You can use a variety of things as a block. Things with an interesting shape or texture, like leaves, sponges and toy blocks, can be used as is. Others, such as erasers, linoleum and wood, need to have a design cut into them. In Chapter 15, on making cards with children, we also look at potato printing.

A related method is the use of stencils to control where paint lies on the card. I have included two projects featuring this technique to show how you can use one or more colors when stencilling.

If you wish to print directly onto two-panel cards, plan the layout so you can tell where and how the front panels of your cards will be positioned. The diagrams show possible plans. For printing, choose paper or card that has quite a smooth surface, otherwise the paint may not cover the surface evenly.

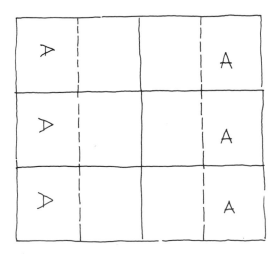

Layout for portrait cards

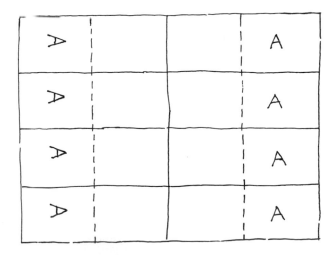

Layout for landscape cards

Leaf prints

You will need:
> *leaves*
> *acrylic paint*
> *a large paintbrush*
> *plain white paper*
> *waste paper*
> *colored card*
> *double-sided tape*

Leaves can be used to create delicate images which are very suitable for greeting cards. When choosing them, look for ones with a well-defined vein system, serrated edges, or some other interesting feature.

❖ Trim any stalks that will stop leaves from lying flat.
❖ Mix up the paint to the desired color and a workable consistency.
❖ Brush paint onto the underside of the leaves, that is, the sides on which the veins are most prominent. Make sure all tips and edges are covered.
❖ Place the leaves, painted side up, on a clean sheet of waste paper and place a fresh sheet of white paper of top.
❖ Being careful not to let the paper slip, run your finger tips over each leaf and stalk. If the paper is quite thin, you will see where the paint is adhering; make sure all edges and veins are well pressed.
❖ Carefully lift the paper, peel the leaves off it and let it dry.
❖ Re-paint the leaves, replace the bottom sheet of waste paper if it is marked, and make another pressing on a new sheet of paper. If the edges of your leaf prints are smudged, try applying less paint to the leaf.
❖ Keep making as many prints as you wish; most leaves will deteriorate only after much use.
❖ When the leaf print is dry, flatten it between heavy books if it has curled.
❖ Cut and score a three-panel mount with a window to fit your print (see page 11).
❖ Trim the leaf print so that it is ½ in larger than the window and mount it, using double-sided tape.

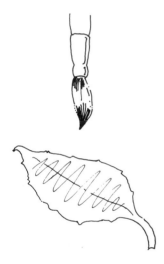

Paint the leaf completely

Press the leaf between two sheets of paper

Eraser prints

Rubber erasers are easy to carve into printing blocks and, as they are not very expensive, are a good introduction to the concept of relief printing. Avoid buying the plastic erasers as they will not absorb the ink well. Pre-inked stamp pads are very convenient to use; they are available in a range of colors.

As an eraser is a small block, it is more suitable for making a repeat pattern rather than a detailed picture. These simple but attractive cards would make good invitations because they are quick and easy to make uniformly.

❖ Mark the shaded sections shown in the diagram onto the eraser.
❖ With the craft knife, cut along the marked lines at an angle so that the unshaded sections are easily removed.
❖ On the other side of the eraser, mark an X on the two corners which have a printing surface; this will make it easier for you to position the eraser when printing.
❖ Press the cut block onto a stamp pad and make some test prints on scrap paper.
❖ Ensure that your paper or card is lying flat on a smooth surface. Plan where the front panel of your finished card will lie.
❖ Ink the eraser block and stamp onto the card. Re-ink it before making each impression and position it carefully so that blocks are printed in alignment and the X marks are in the corner that they should be for the pattern you have chosen.
❖ Allow the ink to dry, then cut and score the card.

You will need:
a rubber eraser
a pre-inked stamp pad
a pencil
a craft knife
paper or card

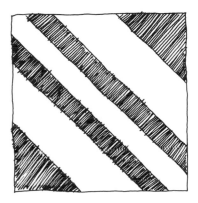

Pattern for eraser block; shaded areas are raised for printing

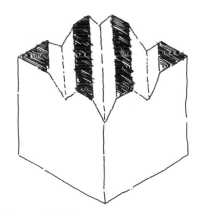

The cut block

Various patterns can be made from the one block

Eraser prints (page 81) and Ball mum lino-cut

Ball mum lino-cut

Using linoleum as a block allows you to create more sophisticated designs, though you will need some specialized cutting tools. These can be bought as an inexpensive set from art and crafts shops, where you can also purchase an artist's roller. You will need a flat non-absorbent surface on which to ink the roller: a sheet of glass is ideal, but a spare piece of linoleum or a flat piece of plastic will do.

This flower pattern would look quite festive if printed in red and, once you have made the lino-cut, it would be a simple matter to print off numerous cards for Christmas.

❖ Transfer the pattern on the next page onto the linoleum using tracing paper and pencil (see page 7).
❖ Warm the linoleum slightly by placing it in sunshine or in a very low oven: this will make it easier to cut.
❖ Cut along the lines of the pattern with a straight-edge cutting tool. Cut so that printing areas have outwardly sloping sides as shown in the diagram.
❖ Use a U-shaped blade to scoop out the non-printing areas between the lines you have cut. You will have better control if you push the cutting tool away from you.
❖ Make sure all the lines on the pattern are clean; the best impression will be gained if lines are sharp and the cuts are at least ⅜ in deep, otherwise any paint that accumulates in the crevices will touch the paper. Large non printing areas, such as the leaves, need not be perfectly smooth.
❖ Shake off the excess fragments from the lino-cut.
❖ Mark up a large sheet of card in pencil to indicate how closely to print. (This design fits a front panel measuring 8 x 5½ in.) Remember to allow room for the back panels.
❖ Mix up paint to the color desired and to a thick but workable consistency, then smooth it onto the roller plate.
❖ Push the roller back and forth on the plate several times in different directions so that it is evenly coated.

You will need:
> 6 x 6 in linoleum
> lino cutting tools
> pencil
> tracing paper
> acrylic paint
> a rubber roller
> a roller plate
> card

Cut lines at a slant and then scoop out linoleum

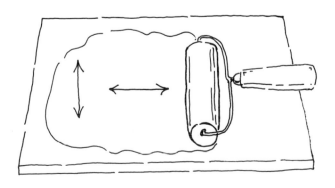

Ink the roller by rolling it on a smooth surface

83

Pattern for Ball mum lino-cut

❖ Run the roller over the lino-cut so that it too is evenly coated.
❖ Position the lino-cut face down on the card and press it firmly.
❖ Your first impression may not be perfect (indeed, a print which **isn't** perfect looks less machine-made) but check to see which sections of the lino-cut need more paint or need to have more pressure applied on successive attempts.
❖ Rerun the roller over the lino-cut and print on another section of the card. If the grooves become clogged with paint, run the end of a paint brush or skewer along them. However, this may indicate that your paint is too thick.
❖ When you have made enough prints, leave the card to dry and wash the roller, plate and lino-cut in water.
❖ Cut and score cards from the successful lino-prints.

If you keep the lino-cut flat when drying it, it can be re-used many times.

Zodiac stencil

Whether or not you trust in astrology, these designs will make very stylish birthday cards for your friends. You might consider making all 12, so that you have a ready-made personalized card when the need arises.

You will need:
heavy-duty card
tracing paper
a pencil
a craft knife
removable tape
a gold felt pen
gold stars
glue
black card

❖ Cut a piece of thick cardboard to measure 4½ x 6 in.
❖ Transfer the pattern onto the heavy-duty cardboard in pencil. (Those zodiac signs which appear on the next page will need to be enlarged.)
❖ Holding the craft knife like a pen, carefully cut along the lines of the pattern. If you slip and make an incorrect cut, stick some tape over it on both sides of the cardboard.
❖ Mark up a sheet of black cardboard for two-panel cards with a front panel measurement of 4½ x 6 in.
❖ Position the stencil over the black card and hold it in place with tape.
❖ Shake the felt pen vigorously to mix the pigment.
❖ Holding the stencil down, lightly run the pen around the edges (if too much ink is applied, it will blur the edges of your zodiac sign) then cover all the area of black that shows through the stencil.
❖ Lift the stencil carefully and wipe off any ink from the underside before positioning it on another section of card to make another image.
❖ When the stencilled image is dry, cut and score the card.
❖ If you have gold stars, stick a trail of them on with a tiny amount of glue. Alternatively, you could draw some with a fine-tipped pen.

Pattern for Pisces the fish
(February 19 - March 20)

Patterns for zodiac signs (not to size)

Aries the ram
(March 21 - April 19)

Taurus the bull
(April 20 - May 20)

Gemini the twins
(May 21 - June 20)

Cancer the crab
(June 21 - July 22)

Leo the lion
(July 23 - August 22)

Virgo the virgin
(August 23 - September 2

Libra the scales
(September 23 - October 22)

Scorpio the scorpion
(October 23 - November 21)

Sagittarius the archer
(November 22 - Decemb

Capricorn the goat
(December 22 - January 19)

Aquarius the water-bearer
(January 20 - February 18)

Zodiac stencil (page 85) and Spring blossom stencil (page 89)

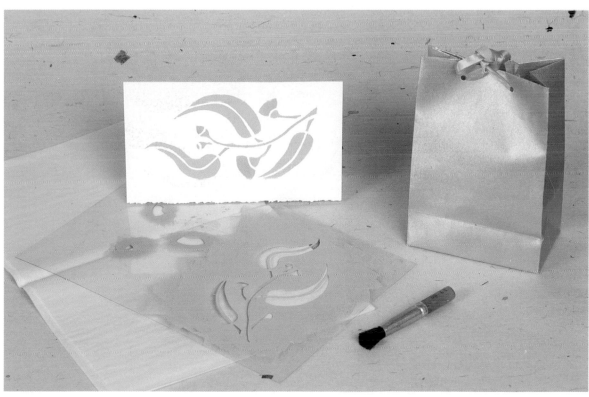

Pattern for Spring blossom stencil

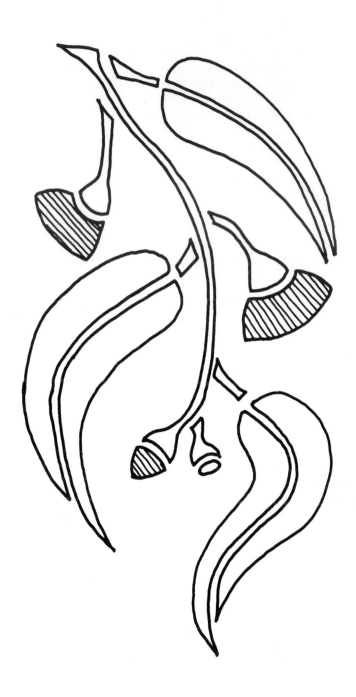

Spring blossom stencil

These tree blossoms and leaves have shapes that make an interesting stencil. When designing a stencil, you must make sure it will hold together by leaving bridges to connect the parts. Blocks of different color must also be separated by a piece of stencil material. When stencilling a two-color image, it is much easier to align each color if you have cut your stencil in acetate. This design will fit onto a single 12 x 8¼ in sheet of strong acetate which can be bought from stationery stores or craft shops.

You will need:
a sheet of acetate
tracing paper
a pencil
a craft knife
removable tape
acrylic paint
a stiff brush
waste paper
cream card

❖ Trace the pattern onto tracing paper: make sure you include the small L-marks, which are registration marks.
❖ Place the tracing paper on a cutting board (it may help to put some white waste paper between them).
❖ Tape the sheet of acetate on top so that one of the narrow edges lies along both L-bars.
❖ Holding the knife as a pen, carefully cut out the sections for the buds and flowers, being careful not to break any of the links. If your knife does slip, stick some tape on both sides of the acetate, or adjust the design to fit the new cut.
❖ Lift the acetate and swivel it so that the other narrow edge lies along the L-bars, then tape it down again.
❖ Cut the sections for the leaves and stems.
❖ Use a pencil to mark up the sheet of cream card into two-panel cards with a front panel measurement of 8 x 4¼ in.
❖ Position the acetate so that the leaf-edge is aligned with the marked 8 in edge of the front panel, then tape it down.
❖ Dip a stiff brush (such as a nailbrush or toothbrush) in the appropriate color of paint and dab it on waste paper to remove excess.
❖ Dab or "stipple" the stencilled area with the brush, using up-and-down movements rather than sideways ones. If there is too much paint on the brush, it will get under the stencil and blur the edges.
❖ When all leaves and stems have been colored, lift the stencil and position it on another section if you are making multiple cards.
❖ Let the paint dry while you wash your brush in water.
❖ Position the stencil so that the other narrow edge is aligned with the marked 8 in edge of the front panel. The buds and flowers should be in the right place on their stems.
❖ Dip the brush in the second color, remove any excess, and stipple the stencilled areas.
❖ Lift the stencil and allow the image to dry.
❖ Cut and score the card.

Layout of pattern on the acetate

12 Needlecraft ❖ ❖ ❖ ❖ ❖ ❖ ❖ ❖ ❖ ❖ ❖ ❖ ❖

Throughout history, people have used a needle and thread for decoration. A wealth of different stitches exists, but a few basic ones can be used to achieve a great range of designs. In this chapter, we will touch on the art - just enough to suggest the endless possibilities that needlecraft offers the card-maker.

Broadly speaking, embroidery can be divided into two types: counted-thread and surface. The first uses stitches of a constant size and shape, such as cross-stitch, on an unmarked fabric. In surface work, the stitches change to fit the motif required, as in the Satin tulips project on page 93. When planning a piece, your choice of stitch will depend on the shape of your design, and your choice of fabric and thread will depend in turn on the stitch. If you want to make more needlecraft cards but would like further guidance, there are many books available that provide details of motifs and small designs.

Embroidered cards may take a little extra time, but you can be sure they won't be thrown out with the gift wrapping!

Materials

You will find it easiest to use fabric with an even and fairly open weave, particularly for any counted-thread work. Several such cloths are made especially for embroidery and can be bought at craft shops and most sewing supplies stores. The mesh of a fabric, such as Aida, is measured in the number of holes per inch: 14-mesh has 14 holes per inch, whereas 18-mesh is finer. A different mesh will affect the size of the motif slightly.

Embroidery threads come in a beautiful array of colors and textures. The most common (and that used in these projects) is stranded cotton which has six threads twisted together. There are several brands of this; I have given the number for DMC shades. If these aren't available, pick a similar shade, or choose a different color scheme altogether. One project calls for you to split the stranded cotton into individual strands.

Select a needle that will not split the weave of the fabric. In counted-thread work I use a very fine tapestry needle which has a blunted point and is not too thick for the weave. Small pointed scissors are essential for cutting threads. Use a large pair of well-sharpened scissors for trimming fabric.

A ring frame can help keep the tension even and your fabric clean, but for small projects it is not essential. If you want to use one, these designs will fit a frame with a 6 in diameter.

To mount your finished piece on a card base, follow the basic instructions on page 13. Generally, a two-panel mount with white backing card will show your work to best advantage; substitute a dark backing card if you have used a dark fabric. Spraying some adhesive on the appropriate panel will hold the fabric neatly in place and prevent it from rippling.

The following projects give a small-scale introduction to several stitches. You might like to try stitching motifs from other chapters, such as the Ball mum lino-cut or the Zodiac stencils.

Geometric curves

You will need:
  stiff white card
  a 60-degree set square
  a large needle
  three colors of thread
  scissors

Here is an idea which lets you use needle and thread without the trouble of mounting fabric on a card. I have used stranded cotton, but any colored thread or yarn will do equally as well. Try sketching different angles and combining them in patterns.

❖ Cut and score cardboard to make a two-panel card with a front panel measuring 5¼ x 6½ in.
❖ On the inside of the front panel, draw an equilateral 60-degree triangle with 10 dots at intervals of ⅜ in along each edge.
❖ Place the card on a rag and pierce the holes with a needle.
❖ Thread the needle with your first color and tie a large knot in the end. It must be too large to slip through the hole.
❖ Starting at any angle, bring the needle up through hole 1.
❖ Push the needle down through hole 2 and up through 3, down through 4 and up through 5, and so on. Continue until the whole curve is complete, then tie the thread at the back.
❖ Thread the next color and turn the card to start again from another angle of the triangle. Repeat this with the last color.
❖ Cut a 5 x 6¼ in backing sheet from white card and stick it on the inside front panel to cover the knots and thread ends.

Sequence of stitches

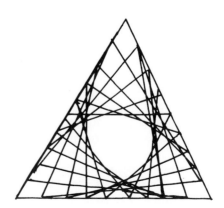

Completed triangle

Satin tulips

Satin stitch produces a lovely sheen when it fills large areas. The pastel colors make this tulip motif ideal to celebrate the arrival of a baby or just as a card for anyone who likes pretty things.

❖ Cut a piece of linen 8 x 8 in (or large enough to fit a frame).
❖ Transfer the design to the fabric. Place fabric over the pattern and use tailor's chalk to trace the outlines. If fabric is too dense, trace pattern onto tissue paper, pin this to the fabric and stitch along the lines of the design with a straight stitch. Remove the tissue and stitch over the outline thread.
❖ Thread your needle with a 12 in length of blue cotton (using all 6 strands) and bring the needle through on the tip of one of the center leaves. Do not tie a knot at the back, but secure the end of the thread by binding it in with your stitches.
❖ Use straight close stitches to cover the fabric, keeping the tension even but not pulling the thread too tight. To finish a thread, run the needle through five or six stitches at the back and snip the thread off close to the work.
❖ When you have completed the motif (and removed any guide threads), cover the needlework with a clean white cloth and press with a warm iron to remove any creases.
❖ Cut a blue two-panel mount with a front panel measuring 5½ x 7½ in and a window 4 in square.
❖ Trim the linen to 4½ in square and mount (see page 13).
❖ Cut a 5¼x 7¼ in piece of white card and mount to cover the back of your needlework. Attach a ribbon.

You will need:
  blue card
  white card
  peach ribbon
  double-sided tape
  scissors
  embroidery needle
  tailor's chalk
  even-weave linen
  DMC stranded cotton:
    754 peach
    794 powder blue

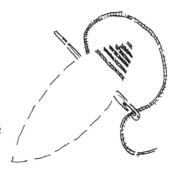

Satin stitch

Pattern for Satin tulips

Satin tulips (page 93), Cross-stitch butterfly (page 97) and Bargello heart (page 96)

Pattern for Bargello heart

KEY:

	mango
	dark grey
	medium grey
	light grey
	lime green

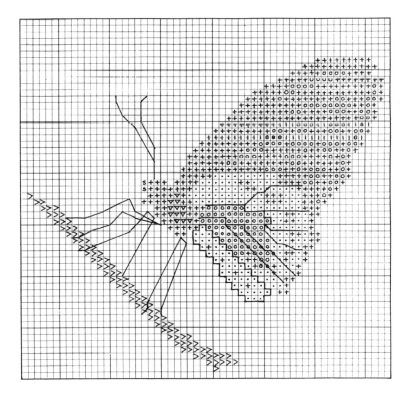

Pattern for Cross-stitch butterfly

KEY:

•	gold
f	black
o	green
∇	red
s	blue
>	brown
/	back-stitch in black

Bargello heart

You will need:
- *grey card*
- *white card*
- *double-sided tape*
- *scissors*
- *tapestry needle*
- *18-mesh Aida cloth*
- *DMC stranded cotton:*
  - *552 mango*
  - *451 dark grey*
  - *452 medium grey*
  - *453 light grey*
  - *472 lime green*

Bargello is a style of counted-thread work that uses long straight stitches in a rising or falling pattern. Because each stitch covers more than one thread at a time bargello quickly covers the fabric, but it is important to count the threads carefully. For this design, use the full 6 strands of the cotton to get a rich effect.

❖ Cut a piece of Aida 8 x 8 in (or large enough to fit a frame).
❖ Thread a 12 in length of dark grey cotton and bring it through from the back at the center of the fabric.
❖ Follow the diagrams for making the first few stitches. Do not tie a knot at the back, but secure the thread by binding it in with your stitches. When you finish a section, run the needle through five or six stitches at the back and then snip the thread off close to the work.
❖ Follow the pattern, changing color where indicated and ensuring that all stitches in the heart are the same length.
❖ Stitch the border around the heart with stitches covering three threads each. Complete one color at a time, sewing the three stitches and then jumping seven holes across to the next block of color.
❖ If necessary, cover your needlework with a clean white cloth and press with a warm iron.
❖ Cut a grey two-panel mount with front panel measuring 4¾ x 6½ in. Measure your needlework from border to border and cut a window in the front panel to fit.
❖ Trim the Aida to overlap the window by ½ in on each side and mount as shown on page 13.
❖ Cut a 4½ x 6¼ inch white backing panel and cover the back of your needlework.

Rising stitches for bargello pattern

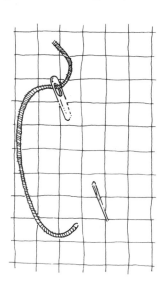
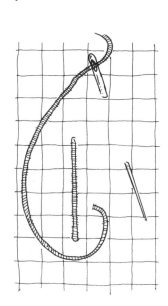
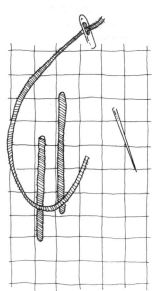

Cross-stitch butterfly

Cross-stitch has become very popular in the last few years and is very simple to master. Each stitch covers one thread of fabric, so it is easy to count stitches on a graph and then on your fabric. This is a relatively demanding design; if you are new to cross-stitching try stitching a couple of rows as practice first. To gain the best results, work the crosses so that all top stitches lie at the same angle. The design depicts the colorful birdwing butterfly (Ornithoptera priamus), found in tropical conditions.

You will need:
    cream card
    double-sided tape
    scissors
    18-mesh Aida cloth
    DMC stranded cotton:
        350 red
        436 brown
        792 blue
        912 green
        973 gold
        310 black

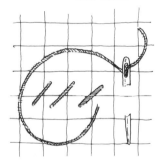

❖ Cut a 8½ in square piece of Aida.

❖ Cut a 12 in length of gold cotton and unravel it into 6 separate threads. (The whole design is worked in single threads to give a finer result.)

❖ Thread the needle with a single strand and bring it up though the center point of the fabric (the top left of the gold block is approximately the center). Do not tie a knot at the back, but secure the end by trapping it with later stitches.

❖ Stitch a series of bars from left to right, then at the end of the row, return by stitching the top bars.

❖ Check the pattern and drop to the bottom of the next row where that color appears, then stitch the required number of crosses on that row.

❖ Complete blocks of color, jumping short distances where necessary. When you need to finish off a thread, secure it at the back by running it under five or six stitches and snipping it off close to the fabric.

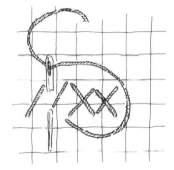

❖ If you want to jump large distances between blocks of the same color, secure it at the back by running under the occasional stitch.

❖ When all the cross-stitches are complete, back-stitch the butterfly's legs and antennae with a single strand of black. Do not jump across from the tip of one antenna to the other: the stitch will show through later.

A row of cross-stitches

❖ Backstitch the wing divisions and around the body.

❖ Cover the completed needlework with a clean white cloth and press with a warm iron.

❖ Cut a three-panel mount with a front panel measuring 6 in square (see page 11).

❖ On the inside middle panel, draw and cut a circular window measuring 4 inches in diameter.

❖ Trim the Aida to a 5 in square and mount (see page 13).

❖ To emboss a line around the window you will need a bowl or jar lid approximately 4½ inches in diameter. Place it on the front panel so that it is an equal distance from each edge and run a tapestry needle (or suitable blunt instrument) around it.

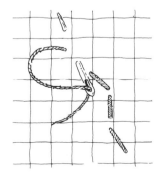

Back-stitch

A sprung frame (page 100) and a three-panel mount

13 Photo Images ❖ ❖ ❖ ❖ ❖ ❖ ❖ ❖ ❖ ❖ ❖

Photographic paper offers a whole realm of card possibilities. A simple photo portrait is a perfect update for distant family and friends, while a creative use of the medium can give new perspectives on familiar places and objects. This chapter suggests a few ways of tapping that potential.

One setback is that photographic methods must increase the cost of your cards. However, whether you're paying for processing or buying your own chemicals and paper, the cost per card will be reduced as you make more copies.

If you can find a cheap source of processing, you might consider combining photography with some of the other techniques in this book. You could, for example, make a complex paper appliqué picture, photograph it and stick the prints on multiple cards.

Many processing outlets provide two sets of prints at little extra cost. Consider spare prints as you would any other printed material; they may make an interesting collage or pattern if cut and rearranged.

Framed photos

When planning to mount a photograph on a card, consider whether it should be removable or permanently attached. The easiest method is simply to stick the print on a two-panel card with glue or double-sided tape. If you think the receiver of the card may wish to remove it, you could use self-adhesive transparent photo-corners, which are available from photographic shops and some stationery stores.

A more attractive, but also permanent, method of framing is to use a three-panel mount with a window cut to fit the picture. See page 11 for instructions on making these. Don't assume that the whole print needs to be revealed: first look closely at it and see if it would be improved by trimming one or more sides. Choose a window shape that focuses the eye on the best features of the photograph. Finally, select card in a color and texture that adds to the picture's qualities.

Another option is a sprung frame, which folds around a photo, giving you a space to write a greeting and allowing the photo to be removed undamaged. Some card will be too stiff to be folded, but choose a paper that will bear the weight of a print. Paper that has been decorated by spattering or marbling is ideal: it has been strengthened by paint and adds interest.

Cut card to size

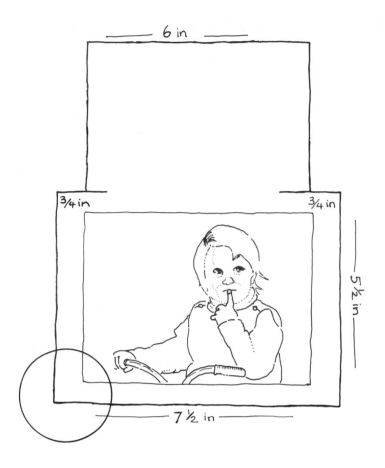

6 in

¾ in   ¾ in

5½ in

7 ½ in

Sprung frame

You will need:
a pencil
a ruler
a craft knife
a photograph
thin card or stiff paper

The measurements given assume that your prints measure 4 x 6 in. If this isn't the case, simply make the back panel the same size as your print and the front panel ¾ in wider and ¾ in longer.

❖ Cut a piece of card measuring 7½ x 9½ in.
❖ At 5½ in along the wider edge, slit ¾ inch in from top and bottom.
❖ Place the photograph in the middle of the larger panel.
❖ Trim a ⅜ in strip off both sides of the smaller panel so that it is the same width as the photograph.
❖ Fold one corner of the larger panel so that the tip touches the corner of the photograph.
❖ Fold it again so that the corner of the photograph is trapped.
❖ Fold the other three corners of the large panel as above.
❖ Fold back the edges bordering the photograph, leaving the top one until last.

If you wish to write a message beneath the photograph, add ⅜ in to the length of the back panel; the card will still stand properly.

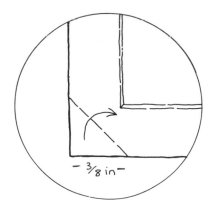

Fold the corner

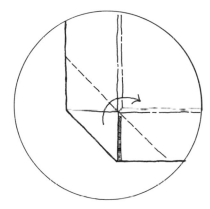

Fold the corner again

Fold the sides and base

The completed frame

Tinted pictures

You will need:
  black-and-white photo
  household bleach
  a dish
  watercolor paints
  a fine paintbrush
  cotton wool
  sepia toner (optional)
  card

Hand-coloring a photograph gives a most unusual effect: slightly nostalgic or quite bizarre, depending on your subject and the colors you choose. A good job requires some patience but no great artistic ability.

❖ Choose a black-and-white photo with good detail and not too many dark tones.
❖ Place the photo in a dish of diluted bleach for a couple of minutes or until the black tones fade but detail is still visible.
❖ It's a good idea to test this on a spare print first. (If you want a really authentic appearance, place the faded picture in a bath of sepia toner for 5 minutes.)
❖ Remove photo and rinse well in cold water, then allow to dry.
❖ Use moist cotton wool to wash in large areas of watercolor.
❖ Use a fine brush to add detail.
❖ Build up areas of strong color by letting each layer dry before applying another.
❖ When dry, mount on a two- or three-panel card.

A hand-tinted black-and-white photograph

Photograms

You will need:
> bromide paper
> developer
> stop bath
> fixer
> a lamp
> tongs
> 4 dishes or trays
> a safelight
> a darkened room
> card

Photograms use the principles of photography to create pictures, but neither a camera nor an enlarger is needed. Objects are placed on light-sensitive paper which is then exposed to light; when the paper is processed, the area hit by light turns black.

You can create striking silhouettes by carefully arranging natural materials (such as ferns or leaves) or man-made objects (paper clips, pasta, jewelry, and so on). Bromide paper and chemicals are available from good photographic shops. Ideally, you need a safelight to see by when handling the photographic paper (normally a red bulb, but ask when you buy the paper). Work at night and, if you have no safelight, turn the main lamp off and rely on light from the next room when handling the unprocessed paper.

❖ Dilute the chemicals as instructed on the containers and pour each one into a separate dish: developer, stop bath and fixer.
❖ Fill the fourth dish with water.
❖ Arrange the lamp so that it is about a yard above your work surface.
❖ With only a safelight on, place a piece of bromide paper emulsion (glossy) side up on the work surface.
❖ Arrange objects in an interesting pattern on the paper.
❖ Turn on the lamp for a few seconds - the more delicate the object, the less exposure is needed. If exposed too long, the silhouette will be murky or disappear altogether. You will become more accurate after a few trials.

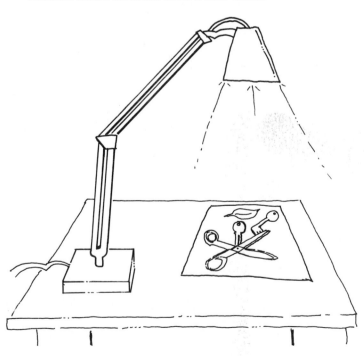

Expose the paper and objects to a small light source

❖ Turn the lamp off and drop the paper into the dish of developer.

❖ Use the tongs to agitate the paper until the image appears and the background turns to a solid black. Do not leave too long in the developer or the image will blacken completely.

❖ Transfer the paper to the stop bath. Immerse it completely for 15 seconds.

❖ Transfer the paper to the dish of fixer and leave it immersed for 2 minutes.

❖ Rinse the photogram thoroughly in the water and then leave it on newspaper to dry.

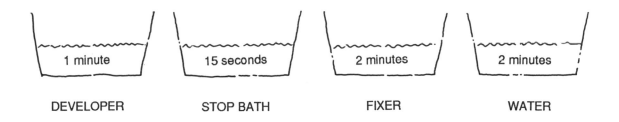

| 1 minute | 15 seconds | 2 minutes | 2 minutes |
| DEVELOPER | STOP BATH | FIXER | WATER |

The sequence for processing photograms

❖ Crop as desired and mount on a suitable card base.

Once you have mastered simple silhouettes, try using translucent objects such as cut-glass bowls. If you move an object slightly between short exposures to light, your photogram image will appear in shades of grey.

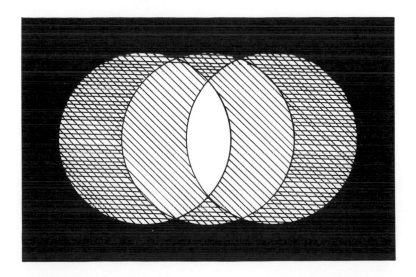

Experiment by moving objects between short exposures

14   Quilling ❖❖❖❖❖❖❖❖❖❖❖❖❖❖❖❖

Quilling or paper filigree is the craft of rolling narrow strips of paper and fixing them in decorative shapes. It was practised as early as the 15th century in decorating religious articles but it became particularly popular in the late 18th century. When Eleanor Dashwood offers to "roll papers" for Lucy Steel in Jane Austen's *Sense and Sensibility*, they are in fact quilling. Originally, the strips were wound around bird quills - hence the name.

It is a particularly inexpensive craft which can produce stunning effects, but be warned: it requires a good eye and a fair degree of patience. Cards are one of the simplest applications - you might use it to decorate boxes and frames, make decorations for the Christmas tree, or even jewelry.

Materials

Some craft suppliers stock packs of specially cut strips for quilling, but you will manage perfectly well with paper that you cut for yourself. Choose paper that is strong enough to hold a shape

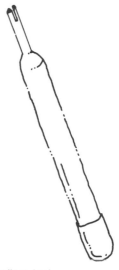

A quilling tool

Chickens (page 109)

but flexible enough to be rolled smoothly. You can get a range of interesting colors from sheets of writing paper, colored streamers, or pads of bright paper sold for children's crafts.

If you are cutting your own strips, use a sharp craft knife and metal ruler, as a ragged edge will spoil the delicate effect.

You will need something to roll the strips around. A rounded toothpick is ideal as the wooden texture grips the paper. Alternatively, there are quilling tools available which have a small slit at the end to hold the end of the paper - this makes rolling easier but gives the coil an unattractive center. You could substitute a darning needle with the end of the eye filed off. The thinner the object you choose, the smaller the hole in the center of your quilled coils will be. The only requirement is that the coil can be slipped off the end of the quilling tool.

White liquid glue is needed to fix the coiled shapes. Only very small amounts are needed so a spare toothpick for applying the glue will be useful. Other handy items include pins, a pair of scissors, some tweezers, an egg carton for sorting shapes, and a damp sponge for moistening and cleaning fingers. If your pattern calls for a number of coils the same size, a washer or curtain ring can help you achieve that consistency.

Cutting the strips

For quilling, the paper is usually cut into strips ⅛ in wide. However, if you are planning to send a card through the mail, a narrower strip will crush less easily. Most shapes require strips between 2 and 8 in. It's important to use consistent lengths when making recurring shapes, so note down the length used. Cut with the grain so the strips will roll smoothly (see Chapter 2 for how to find the grain of a sheet of paper). Use a self-healing cutting board if you have one.

Making shapes

To start coiling, wind the end of a strip of paper tightly around your quilling tool. If you have trouble keeping the paper in place, try moistening your fingers slightly. Use one hand to turn the quilling tool towards you and the other to guide the paper so that each round sits on the last. Coil the paper quite firmly, maintaining an even tension. When you reach the end of the strip, release the coil, slip it off the end of the quilling tool and allow it to unwind until it reaches the size you want. If you are making closed coils, dab a spot of glue on the inside edge to secure it; you can then pinch it into another shape where needed. Refer to the directory of shapes at the end of this chapter.

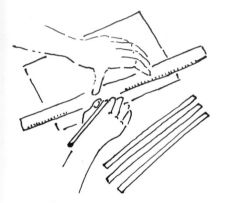

Cutting paper strips

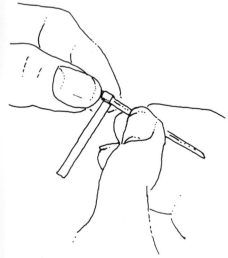

Rolling the strip

Assembling your design

When making quilled cards, you can work in either of two ways. You may prefer to save time by transferring your pattern directly onto the card and sticking shapes directly onto it. If so, make sure you have folded and scored the cardboard before attaching any quilled shapes. Alternatively, you can build the pattern first and then glue it to the card. Try this approach to begin with, as a mistake can be more cleanly corrected.

Trace one of the suggested patterns (or draw your own) and place this on top of a sheet of cardboard that will hold pins. Lay a sheet of waxed paper on the pattern - it will keep it clean and prevent the coils from sticking to it. Roll the shapes required for your pattern, lay them in place and apply glue wherever shapes touch. If the design is complex, pins will help to keep your quilled shapes in position while you work. When all the pieces have been fixed together, transfer the whole onto stiff folded card and attach with small spots of glue on several points of the pattern. Make sure you cut and fold the card base before sticking down any quilled shapes.

A more flexible approach is to simply quill shapes and arrange them on a flat surface to form a pleasing design, before sticking them into place. Different effects can be gained by varying the color and thickness of the paper and the tightness of the coils.

The following projects are roughly graded in order of difficulty. I suggest that you practice making a few different shapes before you attack the more complex designs.

Chickens

This simple design using coils and tear-drops could be given to welcome a newborn baby or to celebrate Easter.

You will need:
  toothpicks
  glue
  yellow & orange strips
  5 x 8 in card

❖ Make 7 yellow loose coils using 4 in.
❖ Make 7 yellow tear-drops using 6 in.
❖ Using a toothpick, glue a coil to each tear-drop. Don't worry if you've had difficulty keeping the shapes a consistent size; simply match heads to bodies of the same proportion.
❖ Take an orange strip and fold it ½ in from the end. Dab some glue on the outside of the fold and attach this to a head (one of the coils) to form a beak.
❖ When the beak is firmly attached, trim it to the right length.
❖ The trimmings can be stuck onto the card as birdseed - cut more if needed.
❖ Score and fold the card to a 5 x 4 in portrait shape, then use a toothpick to glue your quilled chicks onto it.

Sailing boat, Quilled hearts and Snowflake (all on page 112)

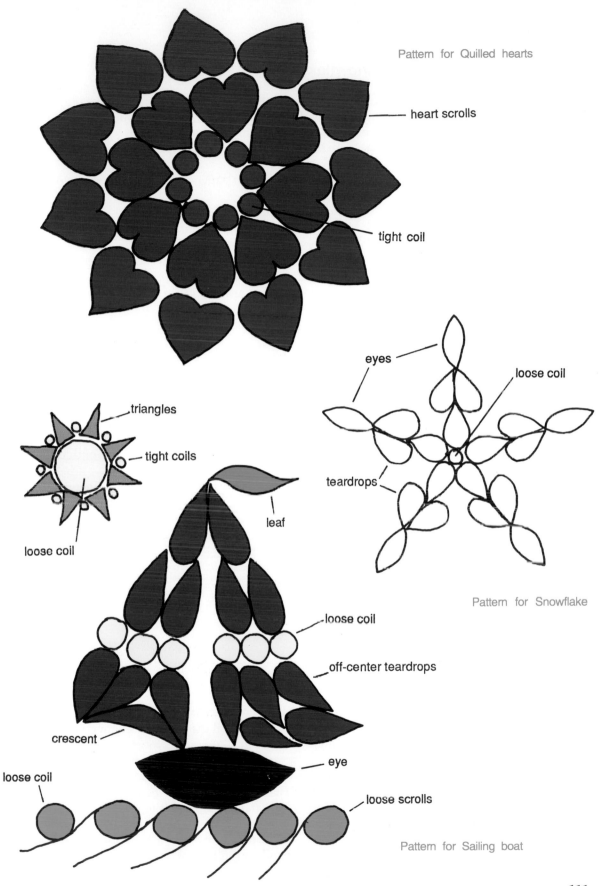

Pattern for Quilled hearts

heart scrolls

tight coil

triangles

tight coils

loose coil

eyes

loose coil

teardrops

Pattern for Snowflake

leaf

loose coil

off-center teardrops

crescent

eye

loose coil

loose scrolls

Pattern for Sailing boat

Snowflake

You will need:
tracing paper
waxed paper
toothpicks
glue
pins
strips of white paper
4½ x 9 in card

Crisp white paper shows off quilling to full advantage, especially against a dark background. This design could also be hung as a tree decoration. One hint: it's hard to match teardrops for size, so measure them when they are still coils.

❖ Trace the pattern onto paper and slip this beneath your waxed worksheet.
❖ Make 1 loose coil using 2 in.
❖ Make 15 teardrops using 4½in.
❖ Make 5 eyes using 5 in.
❖ Assemble the design, using pins to hold it in place.
❖ Working from the center out, glue the pieces together.
❖ Score and fold the card to a 4½ in square, then carefully glue the snowflake in place.

Quilled hearts

You will need:
tracing paper
waxed paper
toothpicks
a thick quilling tool
glue
pins
strips in three shades
5 x 10 in card

This has obvious potential as a Valentine but, if quilled in colors other than pinks, makes a lovely general greeting card.

❖ Trace the pattern and place it under the waxed worksheet.
❖ Make 8 tight coils using 5 in, rolled on a pencil or thick knitting needle.
❖ Make 8 dark hearts and 11 lighter hearts, all using 8 in.
❖ Assemble the design and hold in place with pins.
❖ Working from the center, glue the pieces together. If the hearts don't fit perfectly in a ring, you can stretch or squeeze them slightly when gluing.
❖ Score and fold your card to a 5 in square, then glue the quilled design in place.

Sailing boat

You will need:
tracing paper
waxed paper
toothpicks
glue
pins
bright colored strips
6½ x 9 in card

This bright design will please a child, or make an excellent Bon Voyage card.

❖ Trace the pattern and place it under your waxed work sheet.
❖ Make the sun: 1 loose coil using 12 in; 8 tight coils using 2 in; 8 triangles using 4 in. Glue pieces together.
❖ Make the boat: 1 leaf (the flag) using 8 in; 14 off-center teardrops and 1 crescent (the sails) using 8 in; 6 loose coils (the yellow band) using 5 in; 1 eye (the body of the boat) using 12 in; 5 loose scrolls and 1 loose coil (the waves) using 4 in. Glue the pieces in place.
❖ Score and fold the card into a 4½ x 6½ in portrait and carefully glue the boat and sun in place.

Basic quilling shapes

Coils are closed forms, held in shape by glue. Scrolls are open forms which do not require glue and so have a looser shape.

Tight coil
Roll a strip into a coil, then glue the end of the strip without allowing it to unwind.

Loose coil
Roll a coil and allow it to unwind to the desired size before gluing the end of the strip.

Tear-drop
Make a loose coil and pinch one side into a point.

Petal
Make a teardrop, then bend the point to one side.

Eye
Make a loose coil and pinch opposite sides evenly.

Leaf
Make a loose coil, pinch opposite sides and bend them in different directions.

Diamond
Make a loose coil and pinch sides to form an eye, then push points to the center and pinch the other two points which form.

Triangle
Make a loose coil and gently pinch three corners.

Crescent
Make a loose coil and pinch two points with a concave line between them.

Off-center coil
Make a loose coil, and using a pin, pull the center to one side. Hold shape by adding glue to the bunched-up edges.

Off-center teardrop
Make an off-center coil and pinch the loose side to form a point.

Loose scroll
Roll a coil and let it spring open and remain unglued.

Heart
Fold a strip in half and roll each end towards the inside.

S-shape
Roll one end of a strip to just past half-way then release, turn the strip, and roll the other end.

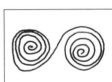

Double scroll
Roll one end of a strip towards the center then release and roll the other end towards the center.

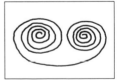

V-shape
Fold a strip in half and roll each end towards the outside.

15 Cards & Kids ❖❖❖❖❖❖❖❖❖❖❖❖

Children are naturally creative and have loads of confidence and enthusiasm to try new methods and ideas. Children also have a lot of spare time and would enjoy making cards, either as an activity on their own or when playing with friends.

Materials

Paper and card are inexpensive materials and can be bought in bright colors with great child-appeal. You might also encourage your child to start a collection of waste paper. Making paper as a family activity is great fun and a good lesson in conservation. A child of 10 years or more could make paper using the instructions given in Chapter 4; a younger child could help, particularly at the dipping stage when the pulp mixture must be stirred regularly.

For small children, a potentially dangerous craft knife can be replaced by a pair of round-tipped scissors. Folds can be scored with a blunt dinner knife or the tip of a closed pair of scissors. Where an incision is necessary (for example, when cutting a window in a three-panel mount) a child can push a pencil or pen through the paper and then use scissors to enlarge the hole.

There are many non-toxic paints available for children's use. Make sure they use water-based paints and wash up right after. Acrylics come in bright colors and an appealing consistency. Powder paints mixed with a flour or non-fungicidal wallpaper paste make an excellent medium for finger painting or for the paste painting described in Chapter 10. Keep a good supply of thick crayons and colored pencils as well.

Choose an adhesive that does not dry too quickly; a flour paste is easy to use and easy to clean up but does not give a very strong bond; the same applies for glue sticks. There is now a non-toxic white glue on the market for kids to use.

Adapting a card craft

Many of the methods covered in earlier chapters are suitable for children to use. Show them the method, rather than the specific project, and let them produce their own motifs and pictures.

LETTERING The best time to learn how to write beautiful lettering is as a child. These days, broad-edged nibs are no longer used in schools, but once your child can confidently form letters he or she might enjoy using a double-pencil or drafting pencil to write in cards.

A simple pop-up construction

CUT-OUTS All projects in this chapter, except for the Advent card, can be made by children though the finished cards will look less sharp if cut with scissors. Children might like to make a simplified version of the Advent card, such as a family tree with windows revealing photos of family members.

PAPER APPLIQUÉ A collage is a wonderful way for children to create pictures; the detail and colors are already provided so they can concentrate on the composition of shapes. Magazines are a good source of printed pictures and if they have kept a collection of different waste papers, it will prove invaluable here. Show your child how to crumple, twist and curl paper into different shapes. For children who are too young to manage scissors, tissue paper is a good material because it can be easily torn.

WEAVING This is great fun for kids. For pre-school children, cut the strips of paper or cloth first and leave them to do the rest.

PAPER SCULPTURE Most children are familiar with paper chains and the starburst can be replaced by any joined design. A simpler method of making pop-ups (which are hugely popular with children) is to bend a strip of paper and use this as a support for an image. See the diagram at the side as an example of this.

PAINTING Paste and spatter painting are messy but very successful with children. Safe wallpaper paste is commercially available, or you might boil up a flour paste and add some soap flakes for a better texture. Children and paint are always a mucky combination, but if you use water-based paints and clean up immediately afterwards this can be minimized.

PRINTING The more basic forms of printing are suitable for most ages, but only children over 10 years or so should be left with lino-cutting tools. Leaf printing is a great activity as it involves no cutting at all. When making stencils, children could use a heavy card and scissors rather than acetate and a knife. This chapter includes potato printing which kids will enjoy.

NEEDLECRAFT The first project, which uses card and thread, can be adapted for small children by wrapping sticky tape around the end of some wool to form a safe needle. Make larger holes along the two edges of stiff card with a hole-punch and a child can sew and re-sew different patterns of stitches. Children aged 8 and more would enjoy working simple cross-stitch motifs on fabric; a good exercise is to form solid letters - perhaps the initial of someone for whom the card is being made.

PHOTO IMAGES Familiar faces in photographs are a great basis for a collage. If you have black-and-white photographs to spare, a child can safely tint them with watercolors, but supervise the bleaching process closely. Photograms might be attempted with the help of an adult.

QUILLING Small hands may not cope well with the width of paper strip recommended for quilling, but if you cut the strips wider - ½ or 1 in wide - children will quickly grasp the concept. Provide an array of bright papers and larger tools for quilling, such as a pencil and the handle of a wooden spoon.

The next few projects are ideal for children; they need only a small degree of co-ordination and concentration to achieve the finished card. An adult might help to cut neater mounts, but a child's uneven finish adds to the charm and such a card will no doubt be all the more appreciated.

Potato prints

This is a good introduction to relief printing; potatoes are a relatively cheap material and can be easily cut with a dinner knife. As with other forms of printing, many cards can be made in one session or children can make sheets of wrapping paper to match.

You will need:
   a potato
   a dinner knife
   water-based paint
   a paintbrush
   card

❖ Cut the potato in half.
❖ To check whether the printing surface is smooth, paint one half of the potato and press it on waste paper. If some areas do not print, slice off a piece so it is a flatter surface.
❖ Cut a pattern by cutting down into the potato slightly and then carefully removing any waste sections.
❖ Cut a handle to make it easier to hold.
❖ Apply paint to the potato block with a paintbrush.
❖ Press the potato firmly on the sheet of card, being careful not to drag it.
❖ Re-paint the potato and print again.
❖ Let the print dry, then cut and fold it into a two-panel card.

Marble trails

Marbles can be bought from toy or general stores. This is a good way to make matching cards and wrapping paper.

You will need:
   marbles
   acrylic paints
   a cardboard box
   a pencil
   scissors
   paper cups
   a bowl of water
   white paper or card

❖ Find a box with a base which measures at least 8 x 12 in (an unwanted cereal box is ideal) and remove one large panel.
❖ Tape the corners to make a tray with secure sides.
❖ Place it on top of your paper or card and pencil around it, then cut the paper slightly smaller.
❖ Lay the paper in the box; it should fit neatly.
❖ Prepare the paint so that it is a thick fluid and each color is in a separate paper cup.

❖ Drop a marble in each cup and tip them so the marble becomes coated with paint.
❖ Lift each of the marbles into the paper-lined box.
❖ Hold the box with both hands and move it so the marbles roll across the paper, leaving a trail of paint behind them.
❖ Once the paper is covered remove the marbles; do not continue too long or the paints will become a muddy brown.
❖ Wash the marbles in water, replace the paper with a fresh sheet and start again.
❖ When the decorated paper is dry, cut and score into a two-panel card.

Drop-dyes

You will need:
food dyes
paper napkins
a cloth
waste paper
glue
colored card

Dampening paper makes it more receptive to dyes and children will enjoy watching the dye creep through the fibres of the napkin or tissue. Make sure the child is suitably dressed; some food coloring will stain clothing.

❖ Place a folded paper napkin on a damp cloth until it too is damp, then transfer it to a pile of waste paper.
❖ Allow a single drop of food dye to drip onto the folded napkin; it will slowly spread.
❖ Add other colors one at a time.
❖ Leave the napkin to dry.
❖ Unfold the napkin to get four squares of patterned paper.
❖ Trim each square to fit a card; these can be glued on a two-panel card or mounted in a three-panel window (see page 11).

Crayon-rubbings

You will need:
crayons
keys or other objects
paper
removable tape
scissors
card

Crayons come in bright colors and can give a lovely textured effect. Part of the fun in this project is looking around the home for interesting objects to use. Anything which has some detail and will lie flat is suitable; leaves with strong veins will give a very good result, as will coins or bits of coiled string.

❖ Decide how large you want to make your card and cut two pieces of paper, one the desired size and one slightly larger.
❖ Arrange objects on the larger piece of paper.
❖ Lay the other piece on top and secure it in place with tape.
❖ Locate each object with your fingertips and rub it firmly with a crayon.
❖ Remove the top paper from the objects and decorate the edges with different colors of crayon.
❖ Cut and fold a two-panel card and glue the decorated paper on the front.

Crayon-rubbing and Drop-dye cards

❖ ❖ ❖ Index ❖ ❖ ❖

Adhesives, 4—5
Advent card, 42—45
Arrangement of message, 30
Ball mum lino-cut, 82—84
Bargello heart, 94—96
Blender, 21
Brushes, 5
Card, 3
Chicken, 109
Children
    card craft suggestions, 115—117
    cardmaking for, 118—119
Christmas tree, 59, 61
Clear impressions, 66—67
Color, adding in papermaking, 25
Copies, multiple, 13
Cotton rag, 21
Crayon-rubbings, 118—119
Cross-stitch butterfly, 94—95, 97
Cut-and-twist figures, 38—41
Cut-outs, 34—45
    adapting for children, 116
Cutting, 8
Cutting equipment, 4
Déchirage squares, 51—52
Deckle, 20
Découpage, 47
Double thanks project, 31
Drop-dyes, 118—119
Embossed letters, 67—69
Embroidery thread, 91
Envelopes, 15—18
Equipment
    for card crafts, 4—5
    for papermaking, 20—21
Eraser prints, 81—82
Erasers, 5
Flat sieve, 20
Framed photos, 98—101
French fold, 9
Geometric curves, 90, 92
Gift tags, 15
Good impressions, 66—67
Gouache, 5
Hearts, quilled, 110—112
Kids, cardmaking for, 114—119
Laminated shapes, 51—52
Landscape cards, 9, 79
Leaf prints, 78, 80
Lettering
    adapting for children, 115

spacing of, 29
Letters
    forming, 28
    weight of, 28
Lines, ruling, 8
Marble trails, 114, 117—118
Marbling, 76—77
Materials
    for children's usage, 115
    for needlecraft, 91—92
    for papermaking, 21
    for quilling, 107—108
Message, 30—31
Mold, 20
Mounting, 13, 92
Multiple copies, 13
Natural perspective, 37—39
Needle, 91
Needlecraft, 91—97
    adapting for children, 116
    materials, 91—92
Objects, adding in
        papermaking, 25
Painting
    adapting for children, 116
    marbling, 76—77
    paste painting, 70—71
    salt and silk, 73, 75
    spattering, 72
Paints, 5
Paper
    fibres in, 19
    handling, 7
    types of, 3—4
Paper appliqué, 47—53
    adapting for children, 116
Paper doilies, 47
Papermaking
    adding color and objects, 25
    materials for, 21
    method, 22—24
    reason for, 19
    varying shape and texture, 25
Paper sculpture, 62—69
    adapting for children, 116
Paste painting, 70—71
Patterns
    for three-panel window, 12
    transferring, 7
Pencil, 5
Pens, felt-tipped, 5

Photograms, 103—105
Photo-images, 99—105
    adapting for children, 116—117
Pierced heart, 56—58
Pop-up swan, 62, 65—66
Portrait cards, 9, 79
Potato prints, 114, 117
Printing, 78—89
    adapting for children, 116
Quilled hearts, 110—112
Quilling
    adapting for children, 117
    assembling your design, 109
    history of, 107
    materials for, 107—108
    shapes, 113
    strips and shapes, 106, 108
Raised découpage card, 46, 48
Ribbons, 5
    tag, attaching, 15
Ribbon weave, 58, 60
Ring frame, 91
Ruling lines, 8
Sailing boat, 110—112
Salt and silk, 73, 75
Satin checkerboard card, 54—55
Satin tulips, 93—94
Scoring, 8
Sculpted flowers, 62—63
Shapes, basic, 8—9
Snowflake, 110—112
Spacing of lettering, 29
Spattering, 72, 74
Spring blossom stencil, 88—89
Sprung frame, 98, 100—101
Stained glass, 34, 36
Starburst, 62, 64
Tags, 15
Techniques, basic, 7—13
Three-panel mount, 10—11, 98
Tinted pictures, 102
Tissue lambs, 51—53
Transferring patterns, 7
True-love knot, 32—33
Two-panel card, 10
Weaving, 55—61
    adapting for children, 116
Wildflower collages, 48—50
Window-box, 34—35
Zodiac stencil, 85—87